'This hard-hitting book uncovers [...] the surrounding world can creep i[...] his years of experience in ministry [...] ...ians identify these pressures to conform. He is particularly severe against different forms of the prosperity gospel, from peddlers of self-confidence to salvation through busyness. He brilliantly introduces us to the historical forces that got us to where we are, but he goes beyond diagnosis and on to the cure: more of Jesus. This should lead to deep antidotes, such as the sense of wonder and a direct gaze at the supernatural. This excellent book needs to be read by every believer.'
William Edgar, Professor Emeritus of Apologetics, Westminster Theological Seminary

'Insightful and convicting, Andrew Fellows's soulful intellect opens our eyes to our cultural moment and calls us home to a life centred in Christ.'
Philip Miller, Senior Pastor, The Moody Church, Chicago

'As Andrew Fellows writes in *Smuggling Jesus Back into the Church*, "When the foundations are being destroyed what can the righteous do? (Psalm 11:3) I cannot think of a more important question for us to grapple with today." Having worked both in the apologetics ministries of L'Abri Fellowship and Christian Heritage Cambridge, and as a church pastor, Fellow is well placed to help us towards answering such a question.

As he explores the relationship of the church of the 21st century with its surrounding culture, his sad conclusion is that even in evangelical churches "the world had become the salt and light of the church" because the church has, mostly unconsciously, bought into the four super-values of modernity: egotism, naturalism, hedonism and politicism. These have replaced Jesus Christ as the centre of faith and life.

Fellows goes on to examine each of these "worldly" super-values in turn, showing what they look like when they are active as the centre of the church, giving a brief history of their origins and ending by showing how we need to "smuggle" Jesus back into the centre of our faith in order to re-orientate the mission of the church to our surrounding culture.

I only finished reading the prepublication copy a week ago, but I have already found myself wanting to give this book to others at least a dozen times. I truly think every seminary student, every church leader, indeed every Christian who is concerned to discover why the church has lost its countercultural impact, and what can be done about it, should read *Smuggling Jesus Back into the Church*.'
Dr James Paul, Director of L'Abri Fellowship, England

'This is both a disturbing and hopeful book: disturbing because it challenges many evangelicals' way of "doing church", but hopeful because it points us back to the centrality of Jesus Christ as the source of a reformed and revived church.

It is biblically profound and compelling, analytically piercing and perceptive, prophetically captivating and challenging. This seminal book is a gift to a church seeking to bear witness to Christ in a secular culture.

Like the sons of Issachar in the Old Testament, Andrew Fellows both "understands the times, and knows what (the church) should do". This book will shake up the church and all who read it.'
Lindsay Brown, former General Secretary, IFES, and International Director of the Lausanne Movement

SMUGGLING JESUS BACK INTO THE CHURCH

SMUGGLING JESUS BACK INTO THE CHURCH

How the church became worldly
and what to do about it

Andrew Fellows

INTER-VARSITY PRESS
36 Causton Street, London SW1P 4ST, England
Email: ivp@ivpbooks.com
Website: www.ivpbooks.com

First published 2022

British Library Cataloguing-in-Publication Data
A catalogue record for this book is available from the British Library.

ISBN: 978-1-78974-343-2
eBook ISBN: 978-1-78974-344-9

Set in Minion Pro 10.25/13.75pt
Typeset in Great Britain by CRB Associates, Potterhanworth, Lincolnshire
Printed and bound in Great Britain by Clays Ltd, Elcograf S.p.A.

Produced on paper from sustainable sources

Contents

To Ranald Macaulay –
for modelling a prophetic courage
to demolish cultural pretensions
set up against the knowledge of God

Introduction

In my twenties, I entered a crisis of faith. The problem was, I was the pastor of a church. Like many young pastors, I found this a heavy responsibility, one I was unprepared for. In my experience, leading a church offered both rewards and challenges, and at first I came through it relatively unscathed. Several years in, however, I began to struggle.

Many Christians go through such moments, wrestling with doubts that sometimes rock them to their foundations. None of my doubts related to the fundamentals of the faith. I wasn't struggling with the problem of evil, or what happened to people who never hear the gospel. Mine concerned the church. I felt torn apart by the uncomfortable tension between how the Bible reflects church compared with what I was experiencing. Surveying the church scene led me to begin to question it, and there were moments when I was tempted to give up on it.

When I turned thirty, our family moved into a different sphere of service. We became involved with L'Abri Fellowship in Hampshire. *Abri* is a French word for 'shelter', and the L'Abri community offered shelter by welcoming people into their homes so they could share life in Christian community that cultivates space for exploration, study and honest answers to honest questions. The first L'Abri Fellowship was started by Francis and Edith Schaeffer in the 1950s in Switzerland, and now there are many more around the world.

After several visits, L'Abri accepted us as workers and our family spent more than two decades in this remarkable community. People came to L'Abri from different backgrounds and nationalities and lived with us, gathered round our table and worked with us in our gardens as we attempted to show and tell the reality of the Christian life. Many came with deep doubts and enquiries about the faith. We listened to their questions, wrestling alongside them for the resolution Christ offered. A good number of our guests were refugees fleeing from harmful experiences at the hands of the church. L'Abri became their asylum shelter as they worked through the ordeal.

Twenty-one years of sitting with disaffected believers sharpened my focus that something was wrong in the church. However, despite my own concerns, I could not escape the fact that the Bible affirms the church's centrality to Christ's purposes in history. For that reason, I encouraged the disaffected to get involved in the local church we belonged to and helped lead. That was important because, despite not being a church or denominational organization, L'Abri maintains a firm commitment to the church.

Since leaving L'Abri, I continue to encounter plenty of disaffected Christians who have moved to the fringe of the church. These include leaders of churches and Christian organizations. And I know many outside the church who see little to attract them. Clearly, something is wrong.

Symptoms of this are out in the open for those with eyes to see. Recently, the church has been rocked by high-profile scandals on both sides of the Atlantic. Christian celebrities have been exposed for serious abuses of their power and the fallout has been devastating. And it keeps happening. The shocking incongruity between what these superstars taught and what they lived has led many to question the reality of what is going on in the church.

There are many other reasons why you might feel weary and wary of church. Perhaps you are a Christian wearied by having to maintain all the programmes your church runs. Between the pressures of home and work we have little margin for much else in terms of time and energy. Churches exert a pressure to serve the cause, and for many this takes us beyond our margins, leading to exhaustion.

Others have become worn down by having to maintain positivity. Their church culture colludes in an unspoken commitment to portray a strong and happy faith. They see this as the best way to market it most effectively to unbelievers. In such spaces there is little place for weakness and doubt. Some reach the point where they can't fake it any more. All the happy-clappy becomes too much and hastens the exit. In my travels I meet increasing numbers who are tired of all the novelty that churches keep embracing. They have gone through so many cycles of doing church – and they have had enough. Others are wearied by their churches stuck in the seventeenth century. These might offer a weighty sermon worthy of one of the old Puritans, but it all seems so unrelated to the rough and tumble of their real world.

On the other side of being unrelated to reality, I hear Christians express their fatigue with a church that makes fighting a political cause the main thing, championing the outlook of the left or the right wrangling with their protagonists. Like many in our culture, they are tired of all the political noise and question it. What have the campaigns of the last decades achieved? Clearly, this contending for the heart of the West has not been a success. Here is a disaffected group who are smart and see the church steadily losing ground and becoming a beleaguered minority. As we lose ground in terms of cultural influence, large numbers are leaving through the back door of our churches – more than many Christian leaders want to admit. The dropout rate of millennials from the church is increasing on an alarming scale.

Of course, there are many churches today with lots to commend them, and when I talk with people who can only see the negative, I gently push back. But the growing weariness many have with church is not without warrant. Something is very wrong.

So, what is going on? This book argues that the diagnosis is a problem called 'worldliness'. It might sound an old-fashioned word, but it captures an important problem. The church has become so much like the world, it has lost its vitality. It is a church that has forgotten Jesus. And how bad is it? No one can tell exactly – but it is a crisis.

Worldliness describes a church drifting from its foundation. It is always a subtle process, and what makes it dangerous is that it occurs without us knowing. What is of concern today is that the whole notion of being worldly has become neglected in the church. That is why I believe this is a critical moment to put in a good word for the concept of 'worldliness'. We need to understand what it is and how it works. We will discover that this problem is not uncommon in the church's two-thousand-year history. In every age and place the church has had to contend with different forms of being worldly. Understanding it becomes more crucial when the church enters a time of persecution.

In this book, I contend that the church must get its house in order – and quickly. This book is a wake-up call to a church that sleeps while a battle rages. Be warned that it is a critique of a significant problem and won't be easy reading. If you are a comfortable churchgoer or church leader, I hope it will shake you out of any sense of complacency that all is well with the church. But neither is it a counsel of despair.

The goal of this book is also to offer hope, and to show that church is worth not giving up on. As bad as things are, we have every reason to hope because the church is in Christ's hands. That holds the key to the answer to my critique. It lies in Christ, who is the head of the church, promising to make it good. This is why he must be smuggled back to the centre of the church's vision.

It was years ago that I encountered the phrase 'smuggling Jesus back into the church'. This statement was used to describe Søren Kierkegaard's life mission. He was a theologically trained Danish Lutheran back in the early nineteenth century who quit the church to become a subversive philosopher. Appalled at the state of the church in his country, he was a dissident challenging its worldliness. He did this in the hope that seeing the problem would create the conditions for Christ to become central again – to smuggle him back in.

When the church drifts away from Christ as the centre, we need a shake-up. This exposure can be a shock but is often decisive in facilitating a return. I hope that this book can play a part to that end. I should be clear that my critique is from within. I stand in the evangelical and reformed tradition and, despite my disapproving appraisal, feel loyal to the cause – an insider. My challenge is a broad one spanning churches of different traditions. While running the risk of over-generalization in my critique, I think you will see that I am not just picking on one constituency. As well as having a corporate focus, there is an application to individual Christians. Today, each of us faces a challenge to be faithful to Christ, and that means everyone has a part to play.

If you are in the category of the weary, feeling on the edge of a church you struggle to identify with, this book is for you. I hope in these pages you will find reassurance that you are not crazy, with valid concerns about the present malaise. While identifying with your concerns, I also believe there are essential reasons to stick with the church. Now is a moment to be part of its restoration and I believe we can strengthen the things that remain even as we critique the problem.

I also write for those comfortably engaged with church, active and committed to the cause. We need to slow down and stop moving so fast. My purpose is to challenge our activist tendency by opening up space for some challenging questions. If we don't slow down for these, we may well be working our way into a wilderness.

While primarily written for Christians, whether committed to church or on its fringes, I also have the complete outsider in mind. Francis Schaeffer always saw the church as living before the watching world. Recent changes have brought the church into the public eye in a way we haven't seen for decades. Although this attention is mostly unwelcome and hostile, at least we are visible. If you are a sceptic looking in from the outside and asking what the church is about, I hope in the chapters of this book you will find an answer, and bear with me for parts of it that might seem a bit 'in house'. To be a healthy church includes allowing for a serious critique of ourselves. We should have nothing to hide – including our dysfunction. There is no hiding in this treatise. My hope in writing for the outsider is for you to see the difference the church is meant to make in the world. Beneath all the flaws and problems of the church, there is something deeply authentic to a faith where Christ is central. Following Jesus is nothing less than life-changing, offering a genuine alternative to the selfishness and spiritual poverty of contemporary life.

Whatever 'camp' you sit in, this book questions the church's status quo and appeals for us to become what Christ always intended us to be. For all its many problems – the celebrity culture, the scandal and the politicization – the church remains the hope of the world because it is (or should be) about following and imitating Jesus.

1

What does it really mean to be worldly?

What we call worldliness simply consists of such people who,
if one may so express it, pawn themselves to the world.
(Søren Kierkegaard)[1]

What kind of difference?

If you are a Christian, what do you think makes you and the people in your church stand out in your local neighbourhood? And if you're not a Christian, what impressions do you have of the churches near you and of the Christians who are part of them? Today, the cultural stereotype is that Christians are generally pushy, judgmental or, worse, hypocritical! However, on closer inspection, many might conclude that, despite the things Christians believe, we are rather nice people, capable of genuine kindness.

We shouldn't forget that we live in a society where lots of people are devoted to good causes. Their decency and care of others are more than evident. Driven by concerns that are admirable, they help the homeless and campaign for the victims of abuse and poverty and care about the environment. People like this are often 'liberally minded' and hard to 'out-good'. It is likely that you live near a family like this. They are upstanding in every way. The parents are devoted to their children. Mum provides a tireless taxi service, running the children to ballet and football practice, and Dad takes them bike

---

1 Søren Kierkegaard, *The Sickness unto Death* (Princeton: Princeton University Press, 1941), p. 53.

riding on Sunday. Sometimes when you see them all out together you almost feel jealous. They recycle their rubbish and the children collect for worthy charities. You also know that they support the local homeless shelter by working in the soup kitchen once a week.

But here's the rub: they are not Christians. So, what's the difference? If you're a Christian, what *ought* to stand out about you and about your family or friendship group? Surely being a Christian must be something more than being nice. Yes, it's nice to be nice, but our reputation must go further.

Getting to grips with worldliness requires us to be clear on the quality of difference and distinction Christ calls us to. It needs to be more than just being moral, conscientious people, and the difference in us must be something that Christ alone can account for. Remove him from the picture and it will be impossible for us to be what he intends. If our distinction is because of Christ, then the difference must begin with our internal life rather than a mere focus on behavioural externals.

Christ's call to distinctiveness

In the Sermon on the Mount, Jesus challenged his followers to avoid being worldly. In words all Christians know, he said:

> You are the salt of the earth. But if the salt loses its saltiness, how can it be made salty again? It is no longer good for anything, except to be thrown out and trampled underfoot.
>
> You are the light of the world. A town built on a hill cannot be hidden. Neither do people light a lamp and put it under a bowl. Instead they put it on its stand, and it gives light to everyone in the house. In the same way, let your light shine before others, that they may see your good deeds and glorify your Father in heaven.
> (Matthew 5:13–16)

Here is the key to being the difference the world requires. As the greatest of all teachers, Jesus knew the power of a metaphor and employed salt and light because each has the distinction factor. When your taste buds are accosted by salt, you always know it by the sharp and unique tang it brings. The implication here is that the church is to keep its uniqueness, and that implies not blending in. Take that as a summons not to be worldly! Similarly, when you are stumbling through a darkened space and someone hits the switch, the light that comes on makes all the difference to how you navigate the room. Here again is Jesus' vision for his people to be an illumination that stands out in an unmistakable way.

Also implied in the salt and light metaphors is that distinctiveness makes it possible for us to be an influence for good on the society we live in, adding something that wouldn't be there if we were not present. Many Christians are passionate about changing the world. But in his salt and light teaching Jesus makes clear that this is only possible when there is something nonconforming about us. We change the world only when we refuse to be shaped by the culture we live in.

The implications of what Jesus is saying here is that this process can be reversed. Then the world becomes the salt and light of the church, shaping and conditioning us rather than us shaping it. Now the salt of the church loses its saltiness and our distinctiveness disappears. When that happens, the church becomes worldly.

I am aware that, for many, the word 'worldly' is awkward. If that is you, then swap it for *accommodating*, a word that communicates that the church is adjusting to the world rather than the world to the church. My preferred synonym is *enculturation*. Look up this word in a dictionary and you will get something like 'the gradual acquisition of the characteristics and norms of a culture or group'.[2] That describes what it means to become worldly, and Jesus did not want this for his followers.

---

2 Oxford English Dictionary <www.lexico.com/definition/inculturation>.

Dismantling trivial versions of worldliness

It is important to stress worldliness as enculturation because the idea of worldliness is often associated with a way of life marked merely by external codes and behaviourisms. This has made the term off-putting for most Christians. I experienced this when I told a friend that I was writing a book on worldliness. She looked at me in horror. The very mention of the subject brought back haunting memories of her church as she was growing up.

This was an experience many of us had growing up in churches marked by a legalistic strain. The logic was that if you avoided certain things, you could escape the sin of being worldly. It was common for churches to create lists of what we must steer clear of. Old-time fundamentalists from the southern states of America operated by the adage, 'We don't smoke, we don't chew, we don't go with those who do.' The list of prohibitions included dress codes and the length of women's skirts. Men were to avoid growing their hair long. We were told the kinds of places to give a wide berth: pubs and bars were the devil's playground, and cinemas were palaces of darkness.

The list of embargoes included what we mustn't listen to or feast our eyes on. Hollywood was tainted by worldliness, and in my home church, the film *Chariots of Fire* was the only exception. That is because this film featured the life of Eric Liddell, the athlete who refused to compete on the Sabbath and then became a missionary! As for rock music, well that was the devil's invention! To subject your ears to such noise was to have gone the way of the world. Hence I hid my collection of Pink Floyd albums behind the panelling in my bedroom. And as a general principle, anything artists produced in the twentieth century was suspect and to be avoided for fear of being polluted. There wasn't much literature, painting or poetry in these circles.

In the end, this approach to being worldly amounted to a shallow legalism. It worked in a guilt-based way that made those with a sensitive conscience feel uncomfortable whenever they came near the prohibited. Sitting in a restaurant with rock music in the background was enough to make one break out in a sweat. Churches set all the codes for avoiding worldliness, like the law of God himself.

Yet, when I searched my Bible as a teenager, I could not find the text that said watching a film was bad. It had parallels with the community of Hasidic Jews in Williamsburg, New York City, made famous by the Netflix drama series *Unorthodox*. With their side curls and special hats called *shtreimel* for wearing on the Sabbath, this group functions by a set of external codes designed to keep them from blending in. Like the old-time fundamentalists, these Hasidic Jews commit to rejecting modern culture, which they see as a source of contamination.

This form of rejecting worldliness has largely disappeared. When we see Christians who operate like this, it makes us chuckle as it looks so antiquated. It is, however, anything but harmless: this kind of legalism causes substantial damage. I have met many for whom this was the reason they rejected church.

What is not so appreciated is that the church today has not replaced the trivial version with the true, biblical idea of what it means to be worldly. The church has stopped worrying about trivial 'worldliness', but without replacing it with an equal concern to avoid the worldliness that Jesus warns us against. While it's good that the church has moved on from a legalistic understanding of worldliness, the church ignores the real problem of worldliness at its peril.

Authentic worldliness

So what is the authentic version of what it means to be worldly? If it is not avoiding certain external behaviours, what is it?

My working definition goes like this: being worldly is when the church forgets who we are because we forget who Christ is.

As I understand it, forgetfulness is the essence of being worldly. Failing to remember is an internal matter, not an external behaviour.

5

It happens within our memory, in our minds, and in how we think and imagine. That is why the authentic version is more elusive than we might have expected and why the trivial version is so wide of the mark.

The history of the people of God highlights this kind of forgetfulness. We see this trend repeated through the Old Testament. The Jewish nation forgot who Yahweh was, and that made them lose their bearings. They drifted because they forgot. Psalm 106 looks back on Israel's history of unfaithfulness and is clear that forgetting was the cause: 'they gave no thought to your miracles' (v. 7); 'they soon forgot what he had done' (v. 13); 'they forgot the God who saved them' (v. 21). The narrative poem then tells us about the accommodation and enculturation: 'they mingled with the nations and adopted their customs' (v. 35). They took on the character of something else, and verse 36 develops this by telling us they 'worshipped their idols'. Forgetting God, they found fresh ones as substitutes for the genuine article. This shaped them, and they lost the salt and light factor and turned into a worldly nation.

What it means to be unworldly

A good way to get to grips with authentic worldliness is to first look at what it means for the people of God to be *un*worldly, or, as the Bible calls it, 'holy'. To be *un*worldly was never intended to be a negative affair, putting us in conflict with the good world God has made. As Saint Augustine put it:

> the temporal life that the faithful have in this world is not to be regretted. In this life they are schooled for eternity and, like pilgrims, make use of earthly goods without being taken captive by them.[3]

---

3 Augustine, *The City of God*, Volume 1, Book 1 (USA, New City Press, 2012), p. 31.

Our calling to be unworldly concerns our being set apart to God. What matters most is him. And when he is first in our affections, we become who we were always intended to be – stable, taking on a secure identity, and at rest. That is the highest and greatest good a human can reach.

Looking back to the Old Testament, we see how God wanted to bless a whole nation like this by setting them apart to be his unworldly people. We read about this in Deuteronomy:

> For you are a people holy to the LORD your God. Out of all the peoples on the face of the earth, the LORD has chosen you to be his treasured possession.
> (Deut. 14:2)

The Jewish nation were utterly unique in being selected by God to be his treasured possession. Because of this, they belonged entirely to him, making them different from the surrounding nations. That is because their God stood out from all the pagan nature gods. He transcended this world as the Creator of all things. Nothing in this world was an adequate reference point to represent him. Hence any image of God was forbidden. As the second commandment mandated:

> You shall not make for yourself an image in the form of anything in heaven above or on the earth beneath or in the waters below. You shall not bow down to them or worship them.
> (Deut. 5:8–9)

We can see this reality reflected in the temple Solomon built ten centuries before Christ came. Other nations also had temples where their gods were set up in the form of visual images. In contrast to this, Israel's God was hidden away in the Most Holy Place. Not being of the created order was the reason for that concealment. Jews who visited the temple believed it was a special dwelling place for their God, but a visit was also a reminder that he was not of this world. This experience reinforced that belonging to an unworldly God was what made them an unworldly people.

Being set apart to the God who transcended this world was a call to a higher trust. To be human is to exist with limitations, and we can't help but depend on something or someone greater than us to support our existence. Left to our own devices, we lift up something or someone within this world order and put our trust there. This trust can work itself out in all kinds of ways. In the ancient world it tended to be invested in religion, or in a king. Today, we like to invest our trust in things like the money markets, political ideologies (say, Marxism) or new technologies. To be an unworldly people meant putting one's trust in the God who was not of this world – the One who is truly sovereign and unlimited, able to support us in our limitations.

Being an unworldly people was also to be demonstrated in what was esteemed as the supreme good. The God of Israel made it clear to his people that 'You shall have no other gods before me' (Deut. 5:7). He alone was to be worshipped and adored. Yes, creation is good and beautiful, but nothing within it is worthy of our worship, and to give it to anything of this world is idolatry. When humans confer their highest esteem on what belongs to the world, it is always detrimental. This point is well made by James K. A. Smith:

> Existentially, the problem with idolatry is that it is an exercise in futility, a penchant that ends in profound dissatisfaction and unhappiness. Idolatry, we might say, doesn't 'work' – which is why it creates restless hearts. In idolatry we are enjoying what we're supposed to be using. We are treating as ultimate what is only penultimate; we are heaping infinite, immortal expectations on created things that will pass away; we are settling on

some aspect of the creation rather than being referred through it to its Creator.[4]

What is notable about the Old Testament is that being an unworldly people was reinforced by all kinds of distinction symbolism. Just after the Israelites were told that they were God's treasured possession they were given a culinary lesson in clean and unclean foods. The guidelines were as follows:

> You may eat any animal that has a divided hoof and that chews the cud. However, of those that chew the cud or that have a divided hoof you may not eat the camel, the hare or the hyrax. Although they chew the cud, they do not have a divided hoof; they are ceremonially unclean for you. The pig is also unclean; although it has a divided hoof, it does not chew the cud. You are not to eat their meat or touch their carcasses.
> (Deut. 14:6–8)

To us, the food rituals, the handwashing ceremonies, the mixed-fabric conventions and circumcision seem alien and strange. But for the Jews, each of these rites reminded them that God had called them to be distinct and different, an unworldly people. As we focus on the peculiarity of their way of life it is easy to miss the main point. Their difference was not primarily because of the external marks of their peculiar customs. It was because they belonged to the Lord, the Maker of heaven and earth.

Unworldliness for the New Testament church

With the church in the New Testament there is a clear carry-over of the need to be unworldly. We see this as Peter describes the church

---

4 James K. A. Smith, *On the Road with Saint Augustine: A Real-World Spirituality for Restless Hearts* (Grand Rapids: Brazos Press, 2019), p. 77.

using words like those describing the Israelites. As an older translation puts it:

> But ye are a chosen generation, a royal priesthood, an holy nation, a peculiar people; that ye should shew forth the praises of him who hath called you.
> (1 Pet. 2:9 KJV)

Under normal usage, calling someone 'peculiar' is not very flattering as it describes something strange. No doubt there are plenty of people in our churches who are unusual – you may even be one of them! But in the context used in the verses above, this is not what 'peculiar' means. As was the case for the Israelites, we belong to One who is not of this world.

To be a Christian is to be set apart to Jesus Christ. As the eternal Son of God, his origin is not of this world but of heaven. Having been sent by his Father, he has come from heaven to this world to be the human face of the God of Israel. Being fully human, Jesus Christ is the visible display of the beauty of the unseen God. In him we can see the goodness, love and wisdom of God. But all this visibility doesn't change the fact that Jesus is unworldly in terms of his essential nature as the Divine Being. And that makes all the difference to who we are as his church.

In 2 Corinthians 6:16, Paul makes the astonishing statement that the church is:

> the temple of the living God. As God has said:
>
> > 'I will live with them
> >   and walk among them,
> > and I will be their God,
> >   and they will be my people.'

God's residence is no longer in a grand stone and marble edifice but in us – his people. Like every temple, it is all about the One who dwells there. That means he is our centre, the focal point of our corporate life. As Christians we rally round Jesus Christ as our binding for our deepest sense of identity and belonging. And, like the Israelites, being set apart to Christ affects our trust. We maintain our unworldly character by investing this ultimately in him – and not in anything that is of this world. When Jesus is at the centre of our vision, we also have clear focus as to where our supreme good is to be found. Again, this is not of this world but is directed to Christ who transcends creation. Here is where our worship and adoration are to be focused.

What differs significantly from the Old Testament is that the New Testament brings a much greater emphasis on a difference that is internal. All the distinction symbolism that marked Israel has been consigned to history. It is no longer required because Christians have the possibility of being and living a new unworldly identity that flows from being in relationship to Christ. By the work and power of the Holy Spirit, the law of God has been written on our hearts so we can be a visible display of Christ. As C. S. Lewis put it:

He came to this world and became a man in order to spread to other men the kind of life He has – by what I call 'good infection.' Every Christian is to become a little Christ. The whole purpose of becoming a Christian is simply nothing else.[5]

Because he lives in us (we are his temple) and because he walks among us, this is the outcome. So the mark of our distinction is one that shows itself from the inside out. When Christ is the centre of his people, the inevitable outcome is that we become holy. This doesn't mean living constrained and narrow lives. Our differentness is not

---

5   C. S. Lewis, *Mere Christianity* (New York: HarperOne, 2001), p. 177.

because we refuse to smoke cigarettes or drive fancy cars. It's because of Jesus. And in John 10:10 he told us that the purpose of setting us apart to himself was so that we 'may have life, and have it to the full'. That means sharing in his life so we bear the distinction of his beautiful life and character. That is what we are meant to stand out for. To avoid being worldly, we must not forget that our difference comes from him. When we do, we drift from Christ our centre and forget who we are. Then we lose what makes us distinct, and worldliness ensues.

Belonging to Christ and the unavoidable 'in' but not 'of' tension

To be 'little Christs' requires us to live out with integrity being 'in the world but not of it'. We draw this familiar phrase from Jesus' words in John 17:

> I have given them your word and the world has hated them, for they are not of the world any more than I am of the world. My prayer is not that you take them out of the world but that you protect them from the evil one. They are not of the world, even as I am not of it.
> (John 17:14–16)

To avoid becoming worldly requires us to live in a tension, one that keeps our place as an unworldly people. As G. K. Chesterton wrote in his book *Orthodoxy*, 'somehow one must love the world without being worldly'.[6] On one side of this we are clear that our feet are planted on this planet. Knowing that Christ made it and holds it all together is our cue to delight in it. As Gerard Manley Hopkins

---

6 Cited in G. K. Chesterton, *The Essential Gilbert K. Chesterton*, Volume 1 (New York: Simon and Schuster, 2013), p. 58.

reflected in a poem, this world is charged with his grandeur.[7] And as his followers we have been brought into a whole world that becomes our spacious place of praise. Being a Christian is to have eyes open to the glory of Christ as it shines in the created order. There can be no hostility to this world in the sense of it being God's creation.

Another side of our feet being firmly planted in this world is that our mode of life is not substantially different from that of an unbeliever. As followers of Christ we sleep, shower, eat, work, wind down and repeat the cycle. Unlike the Old Testament people of God, the outward appearance of our lives is not significantly different from that of our non-Christian neighbours.

However, while living fully and joyfully *in* this world, we are not *of* it. That means there is nothing in this world that ultimately secures our sense of belonging and identity. On this matter it is Christ alone. This makes all the difference to our goals and ends. To be a Christian is to have found a destination and home in the Christ who is not of this world. That is why we do not belong here. We are at a distance from this world because we have a good in him that goes beyond anything this world offers us. That gives us a peculiar orientation.

Paul is getting at this in Colossians 3 when he tells us to 'set [our] minds on things above' (v. 2). Some read this as a licence to escape this world, but for Paul it was a way of expressing what orients us in the world. Where unbelievers have no choice but to embrace this world as everything – including as their home – Christians don't. Christ in his glorious identity as the Son of God disrupts any sense of settling for what this world has on offer. Knowing that keeps us from worldliness and confers on us the status of resident aliens. This phrase was first used by an early church leader called Diognetus who, as quoted by Steven D. Smith in his book, *Pagans and Christians in the City*, wrote the following:

---

7   Gerald Manley Hopkins, 'God's Grandeur' (public domain).

Yet while they dwell in both Greek and non-Greek cities . . . and conform to the customs of the country in dress, food, and mode of life in general, the whole tenor of their way of living stamps it as . . . extraordinary. They reside in their respective countries, but only as aliens. They take part in everything as citizens and put up with everything as foreigners. Every foreign land is their home, and every home a foreign land . . . They spend their days on earth, but hold citizenship in heaven.[8]

Here we see the tension beautifully reflected – residing here on earth but with a citizenship and belonging that comes from Christ: heaven.

A recurring pattern

It is all too easy for this tension to be compromised. Looking back on history we can see that worldliness is a recurring pattern. The Bible and history show that it is the natural drift for God's people. That is why it should not take us by surprise. Reading through the Old Testament can feel like a constant rerun of a film you don't like. Israel kept losing the plot and backsliding into worldliness. They did this by becoming forgetful of who their God was and of the belonging and identity that flowed from this. Every time they did, they became worldly. One of the most shocking aspects of this Old Testament trend is that ten of the twelve tribes of Israel accommodated so comprehensively that they disappeared without a trace. Another significant element in Israel's 'being worldly' pattern was the impact on the temple in Jerusalem. Destroyed by an enemy and deteriorating into a ruin, the fallout was devastating.

As for the church, we need to know that similar can happen. The nature of this enculturation differs from what we see in the Old

---

8 Quoted in S. D. Smith, *Pagans and Christians in the City: Culture Wars from the Tiber to the Potomac* (Emory University Studies in Law and Religion) (Grand Rapids: Eerdmans, 2018), p. 408.

Testament. Because the church is not a nation with physical land boundaries, our worldliness is not mingling with other nations. Neither do we worship idols, because these are no longer part of the modern world. Instead of idols, we take up with the ideals that drive our civilization. Accommodation in the realm of ideas is raised up against the knowledge of Christ and functions as a substitute for him. When we forget who we are, we forget that Christ is our centre, then we drift away by enculturating to something we don't belong to.

The Old Testament and New Testament forms of being worldly have this in common. When enculturation happens, it always leads to a loss of our distinctive character. In both versions, a 'blending-in' occurs so we no longer stand out with a special God-mark. Rather than taking on his likeness and reflecting this to the world, we take on the likeness of the world. Losing our 'Christ-mark', we no longer stand out with our special distinctiveness and thus the temple falls to rack and ruin. In this book, we will examine what enculturation looks like for the church.

Like a pandemic

When the people of God become worldly, it usually affects huge numbers of Christians. It is not unlike some of Europe's pandemics and plagues in the past, killing up to half the population. When the virus of being worldly hits the church, it spreads across denominational divides, and we see the same symptoms stretching across our diverse church cultures.

Like Covid or the flu, there are many variants of being worldly. Enculturation is a many-faced phenomenon. The reason for this is straightforward. There is no singular shape to the societies and civilizations that humans have belonged to through the ages. They change and develop as time passes. Each has its particular 'religious' commitments functioning with their own standards, principles and central ideas.

Different forms of being worldly in the church's history

One thing we can do is look back on the history of the church and see the forms of enculturation it has already faced. For the early church, the danger was accommodation to a culture historians call the Greco–Roman world. The church existed within the social context of Roman civilization, one of the greatest and most famous in history. Here was a context that was pagan, with no influence of the Judeo–Christian worldview. Only recently established, the church existed within this social milieu as a minority and felt high levels of pressure to conform to the Roman pagan way of life. There were frequent outbursts of persecutions as attempts to enforce this. It was a constant struggle for Christians to remain faithful to Christ by maintaining their distinctiveness.

In the second century, one of its famous church leaders by the name of Tertullian quipped, 'What has Athens to do with Jerusalem?' He was using the name 'Athens' as a metaphor for a way of thinking in Roman civilization based on the Greeks. The heyday of their own civilization produced something so remarkable that the Romans incorporated Greek ideas into their own. What Tertullian was doing was calling for the ancient church to avoid enculturation in the same way. Stay with your God-centred identity symbolized by Jerusalem. Don't cave in and become part of the mainstream under the pressure to conform.

Later on, the church in Europe existed in a very different social context. No longer a beleaguered minority, it now had the majority rule. Everyone was a 'believer' and born into membership of the holy Roman Catholic Church – a church so much part of the 'establishment' that it wielded a political power as formidable as state monarchies. This came with its own form of worldliness because when the church is central to a society you don't have to make any effort to be distinctive. Because the Roman Catholic Church was at the heart of the social establishment, its power became corrupt.

Through the thirteenth and fourteenth centuries, this became extreme and was perhaps the church's most worldly phase through its extensive history. We see this in the Avignon Papacy, sometimes called the Babylonian Captivity. Between 1309 and 1376 there were seven successive popes who struggled to extend the church's role in secular matters. Power became central to the church's ambition, and the reality of Christ was largely forgotten.

Later, this power was used to tyrannize the masses to increase the wealth of the church. One form of this was indulgences, a means of paying the church money to lessen the number of years a loved one would have to suffer in purgatory. This was the cue for Martin Luther to come on stage and nail his famous Ninety-five Theses to the door of a church in Wittenberg in 1517. Luther called out the church on how it had become worldly, setting off the famous Protestant Reformation. It was about reforming the church in both practice and doctrine, making faith in Christ alone central. It was a remarkable time, as Christians recollected who they were as they smuggled Christ back in. This made a tremendous difference both to the church and to the culture of northern Europe.

The danger today

What 'variants' of worldliness pose the danger for us today?

The social context that threatens our distinctiveness is called the 'Secular Age'. The philosopher Charles Taylor has done us a great favour by uncovering its centre.[9] He points out that this involves a complete inversion of the societal conditions of the sixteenth century. Then it was implausible not to believe in God, where today it has become implausible to believe. Our culture has become 'godless' – the first in human history. The Secular Age is a way of describing how our society has spun God out to the margins, making him

---

9   Charles Taylor, *A Secular Age* (Cambridge, Mass. and London: Harvard University Press, 2007).

obsolete. It has a set of conditions for its life that we will examine in the following chapters.

This is the form of being worldly that we are being shaped by today. The contemporary church is in danger of becoming a secularized church. I believe that this has happened today, and without knowing it we are in a moment of serious drift. The centre of our churches has undergone an accommodation and an enculturation that has been nothing less than catastrophic.

Francis Schaeffer called this *The Great Evangelical Disaster*, the title of his last book, which was a timely warning to the church on the dangers of accommodation. He wrote:

> The problem of evangelical accommodation, in the years we have been considering, and especially at this crucial moment in history, is that the evangelical accommodation has constantly been in one direction – that is, to accommodate with whatever is in vogue with the form of the world spirit which is dominant today.[10]

The outcome has been the loss of the church's distinctiveness that comes with belonging to Christ. I believe the situation has become so serious that it is time to smuggle Jesus back into the church. I use this phrase only in an ironic sense because, of course, there is no church without Christ. We are his temple only because he dwells in us. Take God out of the house and the temple has no meaning. I use this for the title of my book, hoping it might shock us back to the realization of who we are. Sometimes we need a shock to bring something back to our recollection. Christ is the centre of who and what we are. How could we forget this and put something else there?

---

10 Francis A. Schaeffer, *The Great Evangelical Disaster* (Wheaton, Ill.: Crossway, 1984), p. 150.

Renouncing every centre that isn't Jesus

If you're a Christian or church leader, you might think your church tradition is immune from such. 'But we have a solid doctrinal basis.' 'My church has the weight of hundreds of years of tradition.' Or, 'We have the genuine life of the Holy Spirit working among us.' You consider your church, and it seems clear you are all about Jesus. He gets plenty of airtime. Surely this doesn't apply to you?

Don't forget that it is possible to give mere lip service to something and lose the reality of what the words signify. The Bible warns that we are in constant danger of drifting away from our centre. That is what the book of Hebrews is all about. Hebrews 2:1 reminds us, 'We must pay the most careful attention, therefore, to what we have heard, so that we do not drift away.' There can be no place for complacency, and if that describes our state – we are smug in our sense of being just fine – then that is a warning sign of our being worldly.

It is hard to read the Bible with the matter of being worldly in mind and to resist the conclusion that it is the church's default orientation. Why else would it be one of the Bible's front-to-back themes? The people of God are always drifting towards *forgetting who we are because we have forgotten who Christ is.*

The way worldliness works means there's no room for complacency. We must be on guard concerning good and legitimate things that can replace Christ as the centre ground. It's scary how even excellent things can make us forget our true centre. Today, if you look at faithful, Bible-believing churches, we can see various trends that lead them to drift from their centre in Christ. In and of themselves, the things they treasure are important and require a place in the church to function well. The problem is when they become central.

Here is a list of things that can detract from Christ at the centre.

1 Behaviour

Some churches do this by bringing their codes of conduct into the foreground. I call these the **behavioural churches** – the kind that first trivialized being worldly. The irony is that churches that define themselves legalistically against the world are themselves suffering from a form of worldliness! Rather than relationship to Christ being central, they make various prohibitions the principal thing. These take the form of negatives as the distinguishing mark. We don't have sex before marriage. We are against same-sex attraction and same-sex marriage. We don't let our children go to state schools. We are against modern forms of worship.

Some of these negatives are legitimate according to the rule of Christ. However, when enshrined as codes of what the church is, they can become foreground matters while Christ slips into the background.

2 Doctrine

Other churches do it by making solid theology the paramount concern, so it becomes all about correct doctrine. I call these the **sound churches**, which tend to come from Reformed circles. Of course, it is important that sound doctrine shapes our thinking. However, this can easily slide into the need to be right, and one can hold right doctrine in a graceless manner, contradicting what Christ calls us to be. Sound doctrine can become so central to some churches that the reality of Christ recedes. This means the person to whom all the theology points is forgotten.

3 Experience

Another type of evangelical church – one that has become a vast movement in the rise of the Pentecostals and charismatics through the twentieth century – makes spiritual experience its primary emphasis. The sign of being a living church is in manifestations of the Spirit's power, and these can become so important that intense spiritual experiences are manipulated. These can become rather shallow and give way to what I call the **sentimental churches**. Again, experiencing the reality of God is important for the church, but when the experience becomes the goal, it can leave Christ outside.

4 Programmes

A more recent trend in the evangelical wing of the church is the colossal amount of energy and focus invested in growing the cause. We are living through an age devoted to church planting, setting up tens of thousands of specialized organizations all with the aim of strengthening the church and making it grow. While operating from a legitimate desire to see Christ's work prosper, these can make the 'programme' take centre stage, often driven by numbers and success. As they often produce results, the church becomes ever more enamoured, so Christ gets left behind. I call these the **pragmatic churches**.

5 Ritual

Another trend today is a renewed interest in tradition among those weary with contemporary church. I even meet non-Christians who express a desire for the church to return to its more traditional roots. Wearied by the shallowness of church, many believers are looking for something weightier. Peering into the past, they borrow from the ancient tradition and older institutions using their liturgies and rites to inject fresh life. I call these the **ritualistic churches**.

Again, there is something here to be commended, and my own inclinations lean in that direction. But these rituals can become the central focus, with the danger of putting something other than Christ in the centre.

The double-sided wisdom of an unworldly church

Before we uncover the threat of worldliness today, we should step back for a moment and ask what the church can do to avoid being enculturated. Here I am looking for an approach that works for the church in every age and in every social context. To not be worldly requires the church to commit to a double-sided wisdom – knowing the world and knowing Christ. It is essential that we commit to both/ and – not either/or.

Knowing the world

The first knowing considers the world we live in. We must discern what poses the danger of our enculturation. Every church is set within a social environment, and that environment is the battleground. Not everything about the society we belong to is bad, and much of it exists according to the design of the Creator. Humans are creatures who live in groups, and these groups have their own characteristics. We belong to a group that comprises our family. We also belong to a group that makes up our local community. On a larger scale, we belong to a group that encompasses nationhood. All this is proper and how God made things. However, as we shall see in the next chapter, there is something about our social environment that is bent and twisted. It operates with binding agreements that stand against the knowledge of God. These threaten forgetfulness of who we are. We need to spot where the danger lurks and be on our guard against it. We must alert ourselves to the social factors that erode our distinctiveness.

Knowing the world like this is never easy and always a challenge. They say you should never ask fish, 'What is water like?' as it is so much a part of their environment they are no longer aware of it. So it is with our social environment that functions within a set of values we cannot see. When we have already become worldly, seeing through these values becomes almost impossible. Having become our habit, it is like the air we breathe. Having made the world our home, the church has blended in, so knowing it is beyond us. At this point, the church is living in a state of blindness.

When the church reaches this point, we can only know the world through a special exposure. That is what prophets are for. This role tasks them with a special mission to 'undeceive' the people of God. What we are blind to, the prophets can see. This involves a knowledge of the world. As the world has become our norm, such an exposure is uncomfortable for the church. It is also why prophets go against the grain. When the church is worldly, it sees its prophets as being extreme – if not on the verge of hysteria. It's easy to characterize them as mentally unstable, maybe because they see what the rest cannot.

With this resistance to anything that challenges the church, the prophet includes the message of judgment as part of the wake-up call. The pushback is predictable. 'Why are you so negative and overdramatic? Just tone it down and then maybe we will listen.' Often when the people of God can't shut the prophets up, they lock them up. No one should take the role of the prophet lightly.

So great is the challenge of breaking down resistance, it is a job for the Holy Spirit. Part of his work is to undeceive us. He is the divine healer who can cure our blindness and expose us to the light of what the world is. Through the ages he remains committed to delivering the church from a state of being forgetful. As he is all about the centrality of Christ, his pursuit of the worldly church is relentless.

By whatever means – whether through our discernment, the exertions of prophets or the Holy Spirit's work – it is essential that the church knows the world.

Knowing Jesus

Alongside knowing the shape of the society and civilization we live in, there is another kind of knowledge essential for not being worldly: the knowledge of Christ himself. If being worldly happens because we forget him, then avoiding it means keeping him at the forefront of our awareness. That is why knowing Christ is the key thing.

This has two sides to it. First, it rests in knowing *about* him. This is what theology is for – meaning the study of God. The Bible is a book in which God has told us about who he is. Through the ages of the church, theologians have organized these into a study of his attributes. These unique characteristics of God are to be pondered by his people. The people who know Christ well are instructed in his divine attributes. Sometimes called the 'Divine Perfections', there is a depth of content here that we can never fully probe. These stretch far beyond the body of insights that science has delivered to our world. As wonderful as these scientific insights are, they're as nothing compared to the study of God and his attributes. There is nothing greater for humans to feast their minds on. Without this kind of study, our knowledge of God will always suffer. As the seventeenth-century theologian Stephen Charnock wrote, 'It is impossible to honour God as we ought unless we know Him as He is.'[11]

It is no exaggeration to state that in today's church this is much neglected, and there is plenty that shows a poverty of knowing. Back in 1961, an American pastor and writer by the name of A. W. Tozer introduced his book *The Knowledge of the Holy* with these words:

> The Church has surrendered her once lofty concept of God and has substituted for it one so low, so ignoble, as to be utterly unworthy of thinking, worshipping men. This she has done not deliberately, but little by little and without her knowledge; and her very unawareness only makes her situation all the more tragic.[12]

But, I hear you protest, Christ gets an airing every week in my church. We sing about him in our worship and talk about him in our homilies. But *which* Christ?

Behind our declarations that Jesus is great and Jesus is cool, there may not be much content and definition of who he is. Tozer's

---

11 Stephen Charnock (1864–1866), *The Complete Works of Stephen Charnock* (Edinburgh; London; Dublin: James Nichol; James Nisbet and Co., 1764), Volume 1, pp. 285–286.
12 A. W. Tozer, *The Knowledge of the Holy* (London: STL Books, 1976), preface, p. 6.

statement seems to ring true today more than ever. The contemporary church gives so little attention to the divine attributes. Rarely does one hear a sermon that talks about who he is, the qualities that make Christ God and set him apart in his nature. If the church will move against the grain of being worldly, the study of God must become central.

There is another, second side to knowing Christ, which is knowing him *personally*. Knowing *about* the Godhead is the crucial starting point. This, however, must translate into the knowledge that is interpersonal. This first knowing leads to the second. We move beyond 'thinking about him' to the reality of knowing him in a relational manner. Having 'a personal relationship with Jesus' needs to be a reality and not just a catchphrase.

Here is where the transforming power of knowledge comes into its own. Because we have thought about who Christ is, because we have meditated on the Divine Perfections, this brings us into the place of *communion*. We become the church who can say these remarkable words, that we know him with a personal intimacy. This is the fuller knowing that he made us for. We can know the Christ who walks among us like this, and he invites us into this intimacy.

There are too few in the church today able to say with conviction, 'I know him and with intimacy.' One can detect that this kind of knowing is at a low ebb. We have lost focus on the centrality of being in communion with Christ and have replaced this with other priorities. Even our activities for Christ can easily become a substitute for knowing him, rather than being done out of the overflow of communion. The tragedy of this is that to avoid worldliness, the church needs to know Christ in this intimate way. It is only in this kind of knowing that the habits of our hearts are shaped, leaving the Christ-mark on our lives. Our distinctive signature of being like him only flows from a knowing that is communion with God in Christ.

Chapter summary

Christians become worldly when they forget who they are because they forget who Christ is. This makes them lose their distinctive character as those who belong to him. When this happens, the church 'blends in' so we become enculturated and cease to 'stand out' with our unique identity that comes from Christ. This is something we are always drifting towards and why Christians must be alert to the danger. The church will avoid being worldly to the degree that we know both the world and Christ according to his self-revelation. It is in this knowledge alone that we can maintain the stamp of our distinctiveness.

Questions

- Imagine the difference being salt and light could make to your neighbourhood. How would this practically work itself out?
- What are some of the central concerns in your church that are in danger of being a Jesus replacement?
- Is knowing the 'world' to guard against being enculturated by it a feature of your Christian life?

Further reading

Dallas Willard, *The Divine Conspiracy: Rediscovering Our Hidden Life in God* (London: William Collins, 2014).

G. K. Chesterton, *Orthodoxy* (London: Bodley Head, 1909).

Francis Schaeffer, *The Great Evangelical Disaster* (Wheaton, Ill.: Crossway, 1984).

J. I. Packer, *Knowing God: with Study Guide* (London: Hodder & Stoughton, 2004).

Steven D. Smith, *Pagans and Christians in the City: Culture Wars from the Tiber to the Potomac* (Grand Rapids: Eerdmans, 2018).

2

What in the world is the world?

> Vision is the art of seeing things invisible.
> (Jonathan Swift)[1]

> Whoever controls the language, the images, controls the race.
> (Allen Ginsberg)[2]

Why is it so hard to escape being worldly?

Back in 2016, Viggo Mortensen starred in a film called *Captain Fantastic*. It is about a guy called Ben Cash who hates the capitalist culture of America and takes his children off grid to the middle of nowhere to create an ideal life for them to grow up in. It all looks so appealing as the family farm and hunt their own food and create beautiful music together around the campfire. But when a disaster hits, it exposes the children to the reality of the outside world, and it falls apart. It serves as a powerful illustration that escaping the world is an impossible dream.

During my years in L'Abri, I spoke to many young adults who had been homeschooled by Christian parents to protect them from the world. They would send their youngsters to L'Abri as a kind of finishing school. Having worked so hard to shield them from a secularized world, our 'shelter' was the next step. And so they arrived in our community all clean and innocent – or at least that's what the parents thought.

---

1 Jonathan Swift, *The Works of Jonathan Swift* (United Kingdom: D. Bathurst, 1755), p. 182.
2 Cited in Jane Kramer, *Allen Ginsberg in America* (US: Fromm International, 1997), p. 86.

As I sat in lengthy conversations with them, it often struck me how worldly they actually were. Despite being sheltered, they reflected priorities, aspirations, desires and a general view on things that were the same as the young people who hadn't been insulated. They were living to make money, to be famous or to raise their own perfect families in a this-world utopia. I also saw that, removed from their parents' protective gaze, many were ill-equipped to handle their newfound freedom and often went wild. The local pub made a fortune! All this isn't to say that homeschooling is wrong. My wife and I educated our children like this for several years. However, we should be clear that, as in *Captain Fantastic*, there is no simple escape from our enculturation. Those who think themselves insulated and therefore immune are living in a delusion. In this chapter, we will discover why.

In the previous chapter, we discussed the authentic and biblical version of what it means to be worldly. This happens when the church forgets who she is because she forgets who Christ is. Doing that means we lose our sense of true belonging to one who is not of this world. When that occurs, we move away from Christ our centre and blend in with our culture, no longer standing out with the distinctive character he alone can give us. This departure from Christ leads to the loss of humility and of a proportionate sense of God's justice (not our culture's). No longer do we stand out for good reasons. Our task now is to ascertain how this happens.

When we look back at the Old Testament, we see that the mechanism for becoming a worldly nation was straightforward. When Israel strayed from God, it was because the religions of the surrounding nations enticed them. They saw something in the religious practice that seduced them into becoming worldly by taking up with their gods. It was a case of god-swapping – Yahweh out and Baal in (or whoever the god was).

For the church, the mechanism and process for going worldly is more subtle. It is not as direct as doing a god-swap. When people who call themselves Christians choose to become Muslim, the church would not say they had become worldly, but that they had 'abandoned the faith'. When the church becomes worldly, it is not a case of abandoning the faith but of losing the vitality of it. The impact is a disordered spirituality where the lights go dim and the fire of the Spirit's work becomes a flickering ember.

The New Testament gets at the medium for how this occurs by utilizing the concept of 'the world'. Here is what makes the church worldly. Jesus uses this phrase in his teaching, and the writers of the letters frequently mention it. John is the most frequent user, and Paul and Peter employ it too. It was an important idea for the 'founders' of the church, and one not well understood today.

What is 'the world'?

So, what is 'the world'? Well, it is not the round sphere we plant our feet on spinning at a thousand miles per hour (what one of the old hymns charmingly calls the 'terrestrial ball'[3]). Often we hear it defined as 'the spirit of the age'. This is more a description of 'the world' than a definition. It makes it sound as if the church is being haunted by some kind of ghost coming from another dimension.

The New Testament writers believed that 'the world' was a clear and present danger, and for that reason we require a meaning with more shape and definition. Thankfully, the New Testament letters use several qualifiers that provide a clue to what 'the world' is. In Colossians 2:8 Paul issues the church with this warning: 'See to it that no one takes you captive through hollow and deceptive philosophy, which depends on human tradition and the elemental spiritual forces of this world rather than on Christ.' The footnoted alternative suggests 'basic principles' instead of 'elemental spiritual forces'. Then in 2 Corinthians 10:2 he references the world's

---

3 Edward Perronet (1726–1792), 'All Hail the Pow'r of Jesus' Name' (public domain).

'standards'. Basic principles, the world's standards, all point towards fundamental truths, core beliefs and key norms that make up what 'the world' is. Add them together and it's about the big ideas and values found in our society. It's the 'modus operandi', the status quo, and what makes our society tick, giving shape to a way of life everyone accepts.

For my argument I am calling these ideas 'cultural values'. When these values work their way into the church, the outcome is always spiritual impoverishment. They change the character of the church.

The world isn't culture

The phrase 'cultural values' alerts us to the fact that 'the world' is embedded within culture. Now that we have linked it to culture, we need to back-pedal for a moment to make some important qualifications. Let me put it as a question. If 'the world' relates to culture, does that make culture a dangerous thing? And like Ben Cash and the Hasidic Jews, should we attempt to withdraw from it?

It is imperative that we don't equate 'the world' with 'culture'. They are related but are not the same thing. If we bundle them together, it will be difficult to resist the conclusion that culture itself is something rotten. In *Creation Regained*,[4] Al Wolters gives us the helpful distinction between culture's structure – which is a good thing – and culture's direction – which seduces the church in a bad way.

Too often Christians have fallen into the trap of questioning culture's structure, leading to dire consequences. Indeed, we should be the first to affirm culture. Why? Because it is not the devil's invention. Go back to the Genesis account of creation and you see that culture preceded Genesis 3 and the fall. God designed culture as an integral part of his creation. We are told that he 'planted a

---

4   Albert M. Wolters, *Creation Regained: Biblical Basics for a Reformational Worldview* (Grand Rapids: Wm. B. Eerdmans, 2005), chapter 2, 'Creation'.

garden in the east, in Eden' (Gen. 2:8). Gardening is a culture-making exercise in taming the wilds and putting something different in its place. I think I'll put an apple tree over there, and a border of hibiscus along that edge with a circular bed of roses over on the south side. Our Creator affirmed this act of culture-making as good, and in Genesis 1:27–31 he gave Adam and Eve the mandate to continue this in their 'caretaking' of the creation.

A wonderful aspect of gardening is that it leaves a transforming mark on the landscape. And that's what culture is – the signature humans leave on the world that wouldn't be there otherwise. Our Creator has designed us with special capacities to act on his creation. Our ability to engage in agriculture is another indicator of the expanding reach of 'culture-making' going beyond gardening. Humans can clear large tracts of land and enclose them with boundaries and fences. Then they till the ground and seed it and from the fruit of the ground create stable conditions for habitation and home. Here is another way humans leave an imprint and mark on the world. This would never happen apart from their intervention. When our Creator gave us dominion over creation, he was empowering us with culture-making functionality. This capacity separates us from animals, and it changes the world.

For those with no interest or background in horticulture, you will be glad to know that culture-making includes many other things! We leave our signature in more ways than we are aware of, down to the hairstyle we cultivate. Like the wilderness, if we leave our hair to do its own thing, we'll get an idea of why the cultural intervention of a human is important.

In the past we used the word 'culture' as a reference to the arts – sometimes referred to as 'high culture'. Here is the human signature in its pre-eminent form. The fact that we can make music and paint and create entire worlds through our theatrical productions and novels is testament to the wonder of culture-making. A loving Creator gave it to us for the enrichment of our human experience.

However, as creatures who are fallen, we can now create and use our culture-making faculties in a way he never intended. But Christians should never confuse unhealthy, sinful culture with culture *itself* as the problem. Culture-making is inevitable for humans, and the solution to bad culture is to create cultures shaped by the grace and love of Christ. Everything points to valuing culture as a gift, which shows that we are fearfully and wonderfully made in the image of a creator God.

Counterfeit cultural values

While we affirm the structure of culture, we need to have our critical faculties engaged for its direction and orientation. An aspect of what humans create as culture are 'values', another significant signature we leave on creation. And what is a value? Well, it is something that finds its genesis in the human mind. It is an idea of something that we cherish as being important, of value. We then shape these values in the social domain in some kind of concrete form. When this happens, the value (which previously existed only in the mind) takes a tangible shape.

An impressive example of a cultural value is democratic rule. This notion starts in thought and is not derived from the natural world. The democratic value was not first observed in a pride of lions or a herd of wildebeest. It does not exist in nature but arises in the creative thinking of humans – allowing everyone a say in who has power in a fair and just way. Rather than being ruled by the few who self-impose their unrestrained power – as with current technocratic oligarchies like Google and Meta – the rule of the people is the rule of the many. This value includes a free vote where everyone gets a say in both selecting and deselecting their rulers. Humans translated this brilliant idea into unique forms of government – with either a parliament or a house of representatives. We then constructed special buildings suited to the democratic ideal in capital cities. So we see the cultural value of democracy taking shape in a tangible arrangement.

Cultural values are a wonderful human capacity. We have been remarkably inventive in creating them, dreaming up all kinds to make life work better for us. They are a powerful tool for how we exercise dominion in God's world.

But we often overlook the fact that they can also be a terrible liability. Under the shadow of Genesis 3, we have been creating them in rebellion against God since Adam and Eve fell. For that reason, we often twist them into something in opposition to God and his design for how life should work. One can see such distorted values in matters such as slavery embodying the value of imperialism, or of unrestrained capitalism reducing people to the value of economic cogs in the machine.

There are different key cultural values that work like this, each posing a danger for the church as 'the world'. When we study 2 Corinthians 10:3–5, we see Paul addressing the matter of destructive cultural values, ones that humans set up together that work against God:

> For though we live in the world, we do not wage war as the world does. The weapons we fight with are not the weapons of the world. On the contrary, they have divine power to demolish strongholds. We demolish arguments and every pretension that sets itself up against the knowledge of God, and we take captive every thought to make it obedient to Christ.
> (2 Cor. 10:3–5)

Did you notice how Paul focuses the church on the battle in the realm of ideas, where cultural values operate? He situates this in the realm of 'arguments' and 'knowledge' and 'thought[s]'. Paul is warning the church that we are constantly confronted with a stronghold of pretentious thinking that requires demolition so we can remain faithful to Christ. To use the terminology of this book, Paul is directing us to the struggle with ungodly 'cultural values'. These are values we create as substitutes for God – like idols. These work against the knowledge of God because they attempt to counterfeit what he alone provides, and adopting these makes us worldly.

Super-values

When we look at our culture, there are some key cultural values that make up 'the world' and pose a danger for the church. Our Secular Age has created some absolute whoppers. Another label for this kind of cultural value is an *ideal* – something seen as a model for humans to follow. Where ancient cultures set up idols as substitutes for the true and living God, modern ones set up 'ideals' in the form of 'cultural values'.

Unlike idols, which take the tangible form of a statue or carving, ideals function as intangible ideas, making them harder to locate and demolish. However, modern societies shape themselves by their ideals. When ideals become the principal shapers of a culture, they become what I call 'super-values'. In Paul's words, they are 'set up' or 'lifted' for an entire society to rally around. This makes them central for everyone, and a 'stronghold' keeping it all together. These kinds of ideals have the three letters 'ism' tagged onto the end of them. In the political realm we see this with socialism, liberalism, conservatism and nationalism – mega ideals presenting a model for how nations should be governed.

There are, however, mega ideals not directly political that also rule our lives. In this book I have defined and will examine four 'ism's' that shape our current Secular Age. They go by the following names (note the 'ism'):

1 Egoism – the super-value placing the self at the centre of everything;

2 Naturalism – the super-value believing that what we perceive
is the fullness of reality;

3 Hedonism – the super-value believing our pleasure is what life
is for;

4 Politicism – the super-value believing that the political realm
is where the world is made right.

I suggest that these are the main variants of worldliness endemic in
the church today.

Before we engage with them, it will be helpful to highlight three
characteristics of a super-value. By doing this we can see how dangerous they are to the life of the church. Paul is not using hyperbole
when he calls them 'strongholds' that the church must demolish. It
calls to mind instances in the Old Testament when idols were seen
for what they were, resulting in a campaign of idol destruction. In
2 Chronicles 34, young King Josiah was commended for doing what
was right in the eyes of the Lord, not turning aside to the right or to
the left:

> In his twelfth year he began to purge Judah and Jerusalem of
> high places, Asherah poles and idols. Under his direction the
> altars of the Baals were torn down; he cut to pieces the incense
> altars that were above them, and smashed the Asherah poles
> and the idols.
>
> (2 Chr. 34:3–4)

Such a demolition job was required because of the danger posed to
the people of God. Ungodly cultural ideals that exist as super-values
are no less dangerous today, and here is why.

Spiritually weighted

The first characteristic of a super-value is that it is spiritually
weighted. Paul is getting at this in the language of a value being 'set

up' as a direct assault on knowing God. He is pointing at something that functions like the idols of old, 'set up' in the ancient temples. The ideals that shape and drive a culture have the same religious character to them.

Let's consider what an ideal is. It's about the very best, something without fault and ultimate. When members of a society set up this kind of value as central to its life, it is because they trust it to work. This is a trust of the religious kind arising from our refusal to trust God as supreme and ultimate. For that reason, we always resort to some kind of alternative version. The Secular Age stands out for creating ideals that function as spiritually weighted values we rely on for making a better social environment.

The global response to the coronavirus pandemic that spread to the four corners of the globe in early 2020 reflected the spiritual weight of a contemporary value. What did world leaders look to for a deliverance? Over and over we were told that we must 'follow the science'. Trusting science for the solution blinded us to other issues with the pandemic, making it a handy dodge for politicians wanting to pass the buck to their scientific advisors for the decisions they had to make.

What this highlighted was a reliance on the ideal of science, sometimes called scientism (note the 'ism' tagged on the end). This idea values the notion that science is the only knowledge that matters and is the answer to all our problems. Covid-19 underlined the spiritual weight of this ideal as we put our trust in it. It was a trust just as religious as that of ancient societies, which, in a time of plague, would have slaughtered scores of animals and offered them to the gods. They did this hoping to appease them so their gods would intervene and remove the pandemic. In place of sacrifices to the gods, we have the great science ideal. While giving credit for providing vaccines, we must also question the faith we put in science.

Any doubt about the spiritual weight of super-values can be answered by noting that Paul calls us to do spiritual warfare against them. The ideals and super-values that drive a society are not harmless but pose a genuine threat.

Socially shared

The second characteristic of a super-value is that the majority who belong to society embrace them. Those who don't buy in will be viewed with either condescension (as with attitudes to the Amish) or with the utmost suspicion (as with Islamic fundamentalists). The reason for the buy-in is that the ideal has become inflated to something that transcends the entire group. Everyone has entered a common agreement that this value is essential for our life together. One way we see this worked out is with different buzzwords that we cherish as unquestionable goods, often without truly understanding their meaning – words like freedom, tolerance, choices and human rights.

Just as ancient societies placed their idols in their temples and gathered round them, so modern societies place their mega ideals at the heart of their common life. When ideals reach this kind of super-status, it is only because everyone has signed up to their authority. When a culture value assumes this prominent place in a society, it becomes like a glue binding everyone together.

It is worth pointing out here that the reason everyone buys in is that a super-value has high-level plausibility. Our society embraces these ideals because it seems reasonable to do so. The mega ideal has value because everyone believes it to be worthwhile. That's why it exerts a high level of appeal. We embrace scientism as a cultural value because it delivers on its promises. From it we gather valuable knowledge and learn solutions to some of our most pressing problems – vaccines for viruses, cures for cancers, overcoming erectile dysfunction, the list is almost endless.

As we critique the key super-values that drive the Secular Age, it is crucial that we don't underrate the plausibility factor. It goes far beyond the gods of the ancient world. Zeus and Apollo may have appealed to the imagination, but they did little to save the people from pandemics. The super-values our age has constructed offer genuine outcomes that work, and that's why our culture trusts them. It is this trust invested in super-values that needs challenging – the 'ism' that makes it ultimate. By confronting the 'ism', we then free ourselves to engage the good an ideal might offer. One can take scientism to task and not discard science. That then allows a healthy relationship with science because we don't expect it to solve all our problems and answer all our questions. Tim Keller sees this as the subversive fulfilment of our baseline cultural narratives. For him, 'the Gospel fulfils culture's deepest aspirations, but only by contradicting the distorted and idolatrous means the world adopts to satisfy them'.[5]

Embedded everywhere

The third characteristic of a super-value is that it embeds itself everywhere. Even though values themselves are hidden – existing only as ideas – they filter down and affect ordinary life. There are almost limitless visible expressions for a super-value within the domain of culture. As the democratic ideal becomes embedded in a concrete form of government, so too do the four super-values under examination in this book. They work themselves out across the spectrum of our cultural life. As 'basic principles' and 'standards', we would expect nothing less. The supercalifragilisticexpialidocious quality they carry leaves nothing untouched. Sometimes they embed themselves subtly, and other times it's in our face with everything hanging out.

The idea of the social imaginary helps us grasp how this embeddedness works. This is a set of values and symbols through which people imagine their social whole. The imaginary conditions everyone to a habit of seeing and perceiving. It is an outlook that shapes

---

5   Timothy Keller, 'A missionary encounter today?', Timothy Keller blog, 9 February 2017, <timothykeller.com/blog/2017/2/13/a-missionary-encounter-today>.

our way of being in the world. This shaping can take place through images fed through various media outlets, and through words and soundbites that also help form how we see things. A current example of this is the rainbow image and its accompanying acronym LGBT. Here is a powerful imaginary that is socially embedded, carrying a message that conditions our cultural viewpoint on issues of sex and gender. The power of this imaginary in shaping our viewpoint is colossal.

We can see how super-values get embedded by looking at the hedonist ideal (to be explored in chapter 5). Our modern social imaginary powerfully communicates that sensory pleasure is of the highest value. This is what life is for, and everything should serve this purpose. As our society rallies round this ideal, it finds a tangible cultural expression everywhere – usually not so subtly. Marketing is a key medium for this super-value, and the majority peddles the 'lust of the flesh'.

Take a typical television advert for something like yogurt. That names the product we are being enticed to consume. As a lover of yogurt, having made my own for years, I get the appeal. It tastes just wonderful! But what is striking about the marketing is that it is not about yogurt. It's about sex! And what do yogurt and sex have in common? Funnily enough, very little. However, because sex is the most potent expression of the hedonistic ideal, advertising often makes a direct appeal to it, to communicate why yogurt is worth indulging in. What is being promoted here is the 'pleasure ideal', and yogurt is a means to it. We can see the same in so many advertised products where the appeal comes from hedonism as the super-value.

No escape

A primary vehicle used to channel these super-values is advertising. The power of adverts is that they both appeal to these values to sell their products, and then shape our desires to reinforce them. There is no escape and, given all the screens we use – televisions, computer screens, smart devices – we are under bombardment. The home is anything but a sanctuary from them, and there is no let-up. That is why understanding that they are embedded everywhere is essential to grasp.

The 'world', as used by the New Testament, is all around us in the form of these super-values. Hence the *Captain Fantastic* escape manoeuvre doesn't work, and homeschooling with the exclusive aim of sheltering our children from the world is doomed to failure as well.

Several years ago, I had the experience of being beyond the bombardment as I spent some time with a family in South Africa in the middle of nowhere. It could not have been more remote. No television signal, no internet – talk about being cut off. It was like entering another world, and being media-free was like a shower – after some days I could feel the cleansing as I began to see the world differently. I could detect the difference in their children, not because they had been sheltered but because a world without media was their reality.

When I was leaving, I had an experience of what a rare space it was when I pulled into the outskirts of Johannesburg on the way to the airport. There before me was a massive billboard peddling a perfume, with a full frontal of an almost naked woman – the likes of which you don't see even in the West. Those innocent children might have been sheltered in their own back garden, but in their closest city there was no escape. Media messages would have bombarded them with the super-values of our age.

To return to the virus image, it's no good putting our children in cultural 'lockdown', because the virus is airborne in the media, and trying to shield them only leaves them with no immunity when they step outside the house. The influence of super-values is unavoidable and seductive.

The contamination of the church

Now we have explained what 'the world' is, we need to ask how it makes the church worldly. The process for this is rather straightforward. It's a simple matter of contamination. The super-values making up 'the world' worm their way into the church and infect us. Christians don't become worldly because they smoke and drink or drop the F-bomb in a conversation. We become worldly when the super-values take over and become the dominant influence on our thinking.

Because of what values are – ideas – this contamination happens without our being aware of it. If we halt our efforts to unmask the values, they will mould the church – and in ways we never expected or wished for. It is to lose the battle in the realm of ideas. The super-values and ideals of 'the world' shape our understanding and begin the process we looked at in the last chapter. We forget who we are, leading us to forget who Christ is. As we'll explore in detail in the coming chapters, this is the root cause underlying many of the symptoms, such as shallowness, ugliness or ineffectiveness, that commonly infect the church today.

It is usually a case of gentle seduction. As we have seen, the super-values have a high level of plausibility, and we can easily fall in with them. When this happens, the internal lives of believers become conditioned by the super-values of our day, and the church becomes worldly. Rather than heeding our call to move against the current of the world, we go merrily down the stream with it. Because this impoverishes our spiritual vitality, the church becomes comfortably numb, with the resistance gone out of us.

The Bible frequently uses the metaphor of yeast to reflect how this devastating process occurs. In 1 Corinthians 5:6–7, Paul warns, 'Don't you know that a little yeast leavens the whole batch of dough? Get rid of the old yeast, so that you may be a new unleavened batch – as you really are.'

Recently I became part of a consortium of sourdough bread makers, who like to think they are the elite squad of this noble craft. The thing I like about sourdough is that it works with wild yeast – not the dry kind commonly used today. When you look at your batch of sourdough, you see lots of activity, but you cannot see the yeast. When you add it to a strong flour, the wild yeast does its thing and contaminates the lot. Like magic, it rises to the size and shape of a proper loaf, and that 'contamination' produces a wonderful flavour. You wouldn't believe some of the exotic flavour descriptions that people detect in their homemade sourdough.

This is a great analogy for how 'the world' works, and it is therefore not surprising that the Bible makes such frequent use of it. Like wild yeast, super-values are hidden and work into the life of the church, contaminating us with their particular flavours. If our churches become programme-driven, it could be a sign that we have been infected by a cultural value that trusts efficiency to get the job done rather than depending on the Holy Spirit's power.

For those of you who are not into sourdough, the virus is another helpful metaphor for thinking through being worldly. Here is something hidden that gets unknowingly transmitted, so it enters the body and contaminates. When infected, it has a destructive impact that touches the whole person. There is something about the world that acts like a pandemic, infecting and contaminating us from the inside out.

The 'world' as used in the New Testament is like a virus in a pandemic, spreading everywhere. Like wild yeast, a virus is invisible to the naked eye. The thing about a virus in a time of pandemic is that it respects no borders, and everyone is susceptible unless they have some kind of immunity. When the church is spiritually healthy because Christ is central, it has antibodies that can resist the virus of 'the world'. When our spiritual life is running at a low ebb, our immune system has broken down and the super-values infect the church, making us symptomatic.

The impact on our love

The vital symptom of being infected by the world's super-values is that the church's love for Christ gets disordered. In his first letter, this is where the apostle John focuses his critique of the church going worldly:

> Do not love the world or anything in the world. If anyone loves the world, love for the Father is not in them. For everything in the world – the lust of the flesh, the lust of the eyes, and the pride of life – comes not from the Father but from the world. The world and its desires pass away, but whoever does the will of God lives for ever.
> (1 John 2:15–17)

Notice how he spells it out in black and white. Love of the world is incompatible with love of God. Our being worldly is a deadly virus because it affects our love in such a negative manner. John shows what the impact is on the internal level in our desires – the lust of the flesh and the lust of the eyes.

This focus on our desires is a reminder that to be human is to exist as a lover. We can only be a lover of someone or something because we have a desire for it. It is desire that makes us reach out for what we love. As Joseph Clair writes in his book *Discerning the Good in the Letters & Sermons of Augustine*, 'one's striving toward the good is a matter of love – of one's will clinging to the good in love'.[6] Those who belong to the world operate on desires that love anything but God. Driven by a love of what their appetites lust after and what is visible, they are directed to something that excludes God!

When John talks about the 'pride of life' as another characteristic of what's in the world, he is referring to the matter of fulfilment. Our

---

6 Joseph Clair, *Discerning the Good in the Letters & Sermons of Augustine* (Oxford: Oxford University Press, 2016), p. 170.

pride is in what satisfies us and supposedly makes us feel complete. Unruly desires looking for satisfaction in the wrong places is what the world is about. As James K. A. Smith writes:

> The heart's hunger is infinite, which is why it will ultimately be disappointed with anything merely finite. Humans are those strange creatures who can never be fully satisfied by anything created – though that never stops us from trying.[7]

When the church looks for ultimate satisfaction in the wrong places, it has a disordered love. We forget Christ as our greatest treasure and the object of our first love. If the focus of the church were on Christ who is beautiful beyond any measure of creation, this would capture our desires and we would love him. There would be no shadow of a doubt in our understanding that 'none but Christ can satisfy'.[8] When the virus of the super-values takes over, we lose this focus and our desire wanders to other places. It makes us seek satisfaction in the world rather than in Christ.

How to be countercultural

The church is strongest when its identity is defined against prevailing cultural values. Faithfulness to Christ requires a countercultural stance to the mega ideals. So how does this work? Here we need to heed Paul and take up the fight against 'the world'. For that to happen, we must be clear on who and what is our enemy. Our combat is not against culture itself, which is a gift from God for the enrichment of our lives. Rather, our struggle is with the super-values that animate and dominate our culture.

---

7 James K. A. Smith, 'Heart on the Run' in *On the Road with Saint Augustine: A Real-World Spirituality for Restless Hearts* (Grand Rapids: Brazos Press, 2019).
8 Emma Frances Shuttleworth Bevan (1827–1909), 'O Christ, in Thee My Soul Hath Found' (public domain).

I should add here that our fight is not against the society we are part of. In recent decades the church has too often attacked this in the 'culture wars'. We lock horns with our 'decadent society' and make this our fight – especially on the political front. Overall, this fight has been counterproductive, not least because we have failed to see that Christ calls us first to keep the affairs of our own house in order. Our battleground on the matter of being worldly must be internal and in the areas of our own life where we have conformed to the super-values of our day. It is only the church that can become worldly. This is never an issue for society which, by definition, is already worldly without hope of escaping it.

We can and must bring a positive influence to our culture, but not by becoming like the world. Being power-hungry and self-seeking – marks of the culture wars – are not how to be salt and light. That's why our fight must engage the super-values as they affect us. Our struggle targets the world of ideas inside the church and examines how and where we've been compromised. Paul is calling us to demolish the ideals within our own temple settings – in a similar way to the prophets calling Israel to demolish the idols set up against the knowledge of Yahweh.

When the church does that, it is being countercultural. This is not in opposition to culture itself or in hostility to everything our society stands for. Rather, it is a stand against the mega ideals that internally compromise us. It is with good reason that Paul calls them 'strongholds', because once rooted they are a devilish thing to dislodge. So we must remain vigilant and make sure they don't take root and become a stronghold. This is what genuine spiritual warfare is about.

As with being worldly, spiritual warfare has been trivialized. Several years ago, when I was visiting São Paulo in Brazil, hundreds of thousands of Christians marched through the city on a beautiful Saturday. They billed it as a prayer march to wage battle against the forces of darkness that had brought the city to the brink of hell. It was in the spirit of taking on an immoral culture. To me, the sheer number of Christians gathered was beyond anything that a nation in Europe could ever hope to assemble. That part was truly awe-inspiring.

Wandering through the city the next day, though, I couldn't help but wonder what difference it had all made. One thing that stood out was the vast amount of litter left strewn all over the place. That throng could have made a visible difference had they carried two bin liners each and filled them. Such a practical act would literally have transformed the city. As for the impact in the supernatural realm, that wasn't for me to judge as I couldn't see that far. I wondered, however, about the impact if they had seen spiritual warfare as Paul did – something the church engages with in the realm of ideas against its own compromises.

Identifying the super-values

To engage in the spiritual warfare that Paul encourages requires two things. First, there must be a clear understanding of the super-values that pose the danger to the church's life – ones that are spiritually weighted against the knowledge of Christ. In this battle in the realm of ideals, the church must know its enemy. When we have identified what this is, we require the second thing, which is the divine power to demolish it.

The first of these requires a careful cultural engagement. We must be like the men of Issachar in 1 Chronicles 12:32, 'who understood the times and knew what Israel should do'. So we must know our culture and the super-values that drive it. This won't happen without thoughtful attention to the times we live in with a view to how we are being compromised. It is a sadness to me that so many churches strong in Bible knowledge are flabby in culture knowledge. They assume that knowing the Bible offers sufficient immunity against the challenge of the world. This is vital, but it is not enough on its own. Shirking our responsibility to engage with culture for the discernment of its super-values will leave us defenceless. Despite some key voices within the evangelical church who have done excellent work in this kind of engagement – John Stott, Francis Schaeffer, Os Guinness, Nancy Pearcey and Tim Keller – the church has shirked its responsibility to know the times. I see this as a failure of the Christian mind.

The reasons for this neglect are complex, largely because of the Pietistic hangover. Pietism was a seventeenth-century movement in the Protestant churches that stressed the importance of the devotional life. This had a strong private focus on an individual's spiritual vitality. No one can downplay that, but Pietism tended towards removing the believer from cultural engagement. It emphasized the devotional at the expense of the intellectual. We can trace the poverty of the Christian mind back to this movement. The privatized focus and the diminishing of the mind left us prey to 'the world'. It weakened our defences, and we lost the intellectual rigour recovered at the time of the Reformation. The church became culturally disengaged, and the outcome has been calamitous.

If there was ever a time to re-engage with culture, it's now. Non-engagement is not something we can afford in our time of being worldly. Taking flight from it by going into the bunker does not work. The church as a ghetto – much like the ones built by the Nazi occupiers in Warsaw to segregate the Jews – will not keep us safe from the world. Super-values, like viruses, disregard the walls we put up. They get through, showing that the ghetto response cannot protect us. That is why the sheltered children who came to L'Abri were no different on the inside from non-sheltered children. Parents cannot shield their children from the world; they can only put a resistance to it within them. It's the same with the church. Rather than trying to escape it, we need to face it.

To do this well requires an ongoing effort from all who are serious about following Christ with integrity. How we engage with culture will take different forms, but each will involve a listen-and-learn approach. For some it will involve a careful engagement with the news. Others may feel drawn to the arts and discern the pattern of the world by visiting galleries. A bestseller list of published novels may be the ticket for another. A good friend of mine did this by watching television soap operas and dramas, such as *EastEnders*. He understood that these stories picked up themes that were dominant in the culture and expressed them.

In the early 2000s, there was a very rapid shift towards the acceptance of same-sex marriage. While this was partly the outworking of cultural debate among the intellectuals, for many this change in attitudes was driven by television drama, through the representation and normalization of gay and lesbian relationships in the media. Paying attention to pop culture helps us understand how the cultural winds are blowing. For everyone there will be a point of entry for an engagement that will enable us to discern the times.

Overcoming with the strongest spell

If we have done the hard work of discerning the world, the church still requires a special power for dealing with our culture's super-values as they take root inside the church. Paul says we have access to this power – a divine one. Our need for this is another reminder of what we're dealing with when we battle the world in the church. C. S. Lewis gets to the heart of this when he writes, 'You and I have need of the strongest spell that can be found to wake us from the evil enchantment of worldliness'.[9]

Doing battle with the evil enchantment requires the strongest spell – one beyond our making. So what is this spell? In 2 Corinthians 10:5 Paul links it to taking 'captive every thought to make it obedient to Christ'. For us that means taking his Word seriously. There is a divine power in the Bible that overcomes the intoxicating spell of the

---

9 C. S. Lewis, *The Weight of Glory* (New York: HarperOne, 2001), p. 31.

super-values. Here we see the importance of what the late John Stott called 'double listening'.[10] The church overcoming the world has one ear cocked to the culture with a heightened awareness of the super-values that drive it. With the other ear we are in constant listening mode to the Word of Christ. His Word is our immunity against the world as it tries to lodge in the church. It is our empowerment to resist the virus, our immunity against the super-values.

It all comes down to our minds being captive to his in the realm of ideas. Our minds are to be shaped by a different set of values – not pretensions, but genuine ones centred on him and what he gives us as his people. Everything that the super-values counterfeit, he is to us as the genuine article. To be in possession of his mind is the divine power to overcome and demolish the world's super-values as they try to domicile inside our churches. And Paul tells us that 'we have the mind of Christ' (1 Cor. 2:16). With his help, we can demolish the strongholds and break out of being worldly with a fresh vision of reality.

In another passage, Paul talks about a transformation that occurs through the renewing of our minds (Rom. 12:2). This includes the renewing of our imagination because we need to see the world through a Christ-centred imaginary. Our way of seeing involves how the Bible gives us a better story through which to understand our place in the world. Here is another powerful antidote against worldliness.

In the next four chapters we will examine the four super-values that make up the Secular Age. We will devote a chapter each to egoism, naturalism, hedonism and the new politicism. No doubt there are other cultural values and ideals the church should be wary of, but these four are, in my view, the ones posing the most dangerous and potent forms of 'the world'. It is important that the church engages with all of them.

---

10 John Stott, *The Contemporary Christian: An Urgent Plea for Double Listening* (London: IVP, 1992).

Although each of the four super-values has a distinct identity, it is important to appreciate that they work together as an elaborate counterfeit of Christ. I find it helpful to think of them as the mythical Greek Hydra, a monster with multiple heads, each with a poisonous breath that is deadly to its victims. These heads were indestructible because if you cut off one of them, it just as quickly regenerated itself. It is the same with 'the world' – multi-headed and hard to destroy.

Each chapter will begin by highlighting various symptoms we can observe in the church today. I trust these will be common enough so every reader can relate. I will then move on to diagnose what the 'virus' is. This will involve uncovering the cultural value responsible for producing these symptoms and will include a brief history and taxonomy of how the super-value works in our world today. With this understanding in place, we will shift our attention back to the church to see that it tests positive – how we have been contaminated. I then finish each chapter by turning our attention back to Christ. Only in knowing him for who he is can the church develop an antibody to this form of 'the world'. He alone is the real cure for 'the world' in the church. We will look at how he challenges each of the super-values and attempt to smuggle him back into the centre.

Chapter summary

We become worldly through the mechanism of what the New Testament calls 'the world'. Made up of a blend of cultural values ('basic principles'), these function as pretensions that make us drift from the knowledge of God. They do this by concealing the reality of who he really is, and act as counterfeits for what he alone provides for his people. When we succumb to the seduction of these culture values, key aspects of our spiritual life become disordered. To avoid being worldly, it is essential that we know the world and how it works in the particular society in which we live.

Questions

- What attracts you to 'the world'? What attracts you to Christ? Which is winning at the moment?
- Given that worldliness is all around us in the culture we live in and the media that bombards us, how can we cultivate distinctively Christian minds and imaginations?
- What is your preferred point of entry for engaging with culture?

Further reading

Albert M. Wolters, *Creation Regained: Biblical Basics for a Reformational Worldview* (Grand Rapids: Wm. B. Eerdmans, 2005).

Andy Crouch, *Culture Making: Recovering Our Creative Calling* (Downers Grove: InterVarsity Press, 2009).

James K. A. Smith, *How (Not) to Be Secular: Reading Charles Taylor* (Grand Rapids: Wm B. Eerdmans, 2014).

Bob Goudzwaard and Craig G. Bartholomew, *Beyond the Modern Age: An Archaeology of Contemporary Culture* (Downers Grove: IVP Academic, 2017).

Charles Taylor, *A Secular Age* (Cambridge, Mass. and London: Harvard University Press, 2007).

3

Egoism: it's all about *you!*

The men who really believe in themselves
are all in lunatic asylums.
(G. K. Chesterton)[1]

When Laura felt dissatisfied with her life, wondering what it was all about, she turned to the usual place she went to for answers: the internet. After a series of searches about finding meaning in life, she stumbled across a YouTube video of a fast-talking, confident preacher from a big church near where she lived. He was engaging and funny, as well as preaching clearly about Jesus and what it means to follow him. Eventually Laura started attending the church in person, which was much slicker and trendier than how she had envisioned church to be. She did a course explaining the basics of the faith and fell in love with Jesus. As she heard about his amazing life and teaching, and how he died for her sins, she become a true follower. Laura joined her church, got involved with a small group and volunteered for one of its many programmes.

But over time, Laura began to feel uneasy. She couldn't fully articulate what troubled her, but she began to notice how the pastor's call to follow Jesus often slid seamlessly into a call to give more time to church activities – to volunteer more, to give more money, to invite more friends to attend to hear him speak. Despite all the slogans about being all about Jesus, in practice it seemed to be becoming more about the church's numbers and reputation, and about the pastor's platform as a preacher. With increasing pressure to conform

---

1 G. K. Chesterton, *Orthodoxy* (London: Bodley Head, 1909), p. 22.

and serve, and a growing sense of something inauthentic, church became more of a chore for Laura, rather than growing her love for Christ and for her neighbours.

Symptoms of a disorder

There is not a church anywhere that wouldn't assert it is all about Jesus. How could it be otherwise? It is unthinkable that a church could have any other reason for existing. We convince ourselves it is all about him – but is it? A closer look may uncover that it is more about us. So ask yourself this question: if someone unchurched were to attend one of our gatherings, what impressions would it leave? If they were to ask, what's this about, who's it about and what's its centre, what would they conclude?

As we think about impressions, we shouldn't overlook the old adage that 'the medium is the message'. The modes and methods we employ are a key aspect of what we communicate. We may give lip service to Jesus, but our practice often conveys a different priority.

Church celebrity culture

Lots of churches today are likely to leave an outsider with the impression that it is about someone who is well known. We have developed a proclivity for celebrities, of the same kind that marks our culture. Mega churches become known as cool for the celebrities who attend – be it Justin Bieber, some of the Kardashians or a sporting icon.

What also stands out in large churches are the celebrity pastors. Treated like royalty, they collude in a delusion of grandeur. Some even have bodyguards to protect them from ordinary run-of-the-mill Christians who want their attention. Their work is too important for that, yet they seem to have time to move with the rich and the famous. As celebrities, they maintain their following through social media and love to be liked as they share their opinions on various current trends. Many church leaders obsess about their CV and bio and aspire to be acclaimed. It fits with an ethos of self-promotion to convince others that 'I am a big deal'.

How this fits with Jesus, who avoided self-promotion, is not considered. It doesn't bear any resemblance to Mark 1:43–44 where, after healing a leper, Jesus told him, 'See that you don't tell this to anyone.'

And, of course, when church leaders cement their reputation and success, that creates the conditions for building an institution around them. Doing that is conflated with building Christ's kingdom. This works because ordinary Christians love celebrities and prop up this culture in the church. Somehow it all feels more authentic if we stand alongside fame and success. As Scot McKnight and Laura Barringer highlight in their book, *A Church Called Tov*:

> Of course, celebrities don't form on their own. Behind every celebrity pastor is an adoring congregation that both loves and supports the celebrity atmosphere. The development of a celebrity culture also doesn't happen overnight. It begins when a pastor has a driving ambition for fame, but it can't take root unless the congregation supports that ambition.[2]

While this celebrity culture is a standout feature of the mega church, pastors of smaller churches can also play this game, doing all they can to improve their profile and public persona. Again, ordinary congregants often expect their pastors and leaders to be well known for something, be it a published book or a trendy blog.

The emotional prosperity gospel

Another observable symptom is something I call the emotional prosperity gospel. People like Laura are told that following Jesus is the

2 Scot McKnight and Laura Barringer, *A Church Called Tov: Forming a Goodness Culture that Resists Abuses of Power and Promotes Healing* (Carol Stream, Ill.: Tyndale Momentum, 2020), p. 256.

better path to being a stable human being. Most Bible-based churches reject the health and wealth prosperity gospel, which promises that Jesus is going to improve the material conditions of your life. There is, however, another prosperity gospel, more subtle and just as dangerous.

An outsider coming into our gatherings would pick up our commitment to human flourishing – one that the Bible endorses. Here are people wanting to be better spouses and parents and citizens making a social difference. Don't forget that many unbelievers have the same goals! They would also hear about living without anxiety and operating from a place of deep inner peace. This is couched in the language of pop psychology that dominates our culture today. It is a little different because of the religious twist. Do you want to overcome your self-doubt and achieve your full potential? Well, guess what, Jesus is your divine therapist and the reason he exists is to make you a better version of yourself. With his help you can master your inner demons and he can empower you to realize your talent and natural gifting.

We are reducing 'the faith' to a self-improvement programme. We see Christianity as the means to finding the better version of you, and Christ's primary goal in life is to serve this end. The content of many of our sermons wouldn't change much if we were to swap out Christ for the modern gospel of how to realize your self-potential.

Leaving our sermons aside, what about the top-selling books in the Christian market? What do the titles suggest for a focus? Millions of evangelicals read books like *Your Best Life Now: Seven Steps to Living at Your Full Potential*. The writer followed up with *Break Out: 5 Keys to Go Beyond Your Barriers and Live an Extraordinary Life*. This book could be described as self-belief ideology dressed up in God talk.

As I write, the titles of some of the bestselling books topping the Christian charts include phrases like 'a journey to self-discovery', 'dream big', and 'drop the guilt and do what makes you alive'. It may be that some of these books genuinely aim to bring Christ to those into self-help, rather than self-help into Christianity. But it's a dangerous game to play. There's a lot of self in these titles and they appear to line up well with current commitments in our culture. This kind of thinking has left its mark and much of our teaching is a form of therapeutic Christianity. Therapeutic faith focuses on who we are and what we want. Even when we bring in Christ, it's still really about us. And so we are in danger of reducing the faith to a Christianized 'pop psychology' in the interests of enhancing our self-potential and bolstering our emotional well-being.

Keeping it positive

Like our therapeutic culture, the church has committed to positivity. Everything about the Christian life must be upbeat and the negative left at the door. We are told we can do all things 'through him who gives me strength' and consoled that the Lord will never give us more than we can handle (Phil. 4:13; 1 Cor. 10:13). This positivity includes how we think about ourselves. Yes, we are damaged goods, but Christ has seen the wonderful potential in us and wants to help.

Such an approach diminishes the Bible's darker assessment about our condition. God's Word sees humans as radically corrupted, and if there is unrealized potential in us, it's the darker kind and our capacity for rebellion against God. Under the effects of the fall, sin is our default condition and why we turn away from God. It means we are naturally allergic and resistant to the One who made us. It is our self-aggrandizement that hinders us from seeing and appreciating his flawless worth and beauty. Indeed, our situation is so serious that the Bible writes us a death certificate – something extending beyond being damaged. Our quandary is so overwhelming that only God can help. It required nothing less than the death of his own Son, and only in this is there a possibility for a new self to live. Apart from such a radical intervention, the old self remains in death.

With our diminished view of sin, we've turned the gospel into something more remedial. According to the therapeutic gospel, Jesus came to rescue us because he saw our woundedness and how we were victims of poor parenting and adverse social conditions. He stepped in so we could become a better version of ourselves. There is an element of truth in this because, of course, he has compassion for our brokenness and commits to improving us. He is all about creating a beautiful version of us. But this comes to pass as we move beyond ourselves and see him for who he is. Our transformation requires something no form of therapy could ever carry out.

The doctrine of sanctification reflects this, with the reminder that it's a work of his grace and power. Nothing less than Christ himself can remake us to the end of becoming like him and not a better version of me. This is at odds with the models for self-improvement the church has adopted today – ones where Christ offers a healing hand on the path to self-realization. If we were to delete Christ altogether from our self-improvement teaching and put in Buddha or the power of 'positive thinking', I don't think it would make much difference. Our therapeutic models do their work without his help – much like the kind of self-help our culture follows.

The activist church

Another symptom is the rise of the activist church – the kind that Laura discovered as she got involved. On a positive note, I would argue that the evangelical church has never been better resourced than it is today – evangelism and apologetics training, church planting and leadership development and a plethora of aids for studying and teaching the Bible. This is a wonderful development. Christians have also become crusaders and campaigners to change the world, and we have so many causes.

When an outsider comes through the door, they might conclude, 'Oh, I get it, it's all about the family – happily married couples who have beautiful children.' Don't forget that Walter White in *Breaking Bad* had the same goal, leading to his descent into crime in pursuit of it. Or they might assume it is about being hipster, being inclusive to everyone, or being a social justice warrior by fighting oppression and discrimination. Clearly, there seems to be a lot going on, but what might not be so clear is how it's about Christ.

We see our activist tendency in churches being structured by programmes. When I travel and sit in on a Sunday morning service, I often reach a state of exhaustion as I'm confronted by the various programmes run by the church. A special initiative for singles – the under-thirties and the over-thirties. It's as if there's a special self-help group for everyone. To the watching world this just seems to mirror modernity – where everything becomes busy and bureaucratic.

Now, of course, to function well as a church requires being organized. It needs a plan that caters for youth work, house groups, and music on Sunday where everyone sings the same worship song to the same tune. It is easy, however, to move from being organized to being programmatical – where everything is led by the programme. Even a typical house group meeting is structured – with set questions and answers, and the prayer time programmed according to a form that never allows for anything different. All the programmes reflect how we have become activist. The issue with our activism is not so much what we pursue but how we realize our plans. We achieve our causes and programmes without having to depend on Christ. At best we ask him for his rubber stamp of approval as we pursue our latest campaign.

A corresponding symptom to all the activism is the scale of weariness that marks the church today. Burnout among church workers and ministry leaders is common and symptomatic of this. Christians come across as harried, rushed and burdened by the weight of their activism. It is my observation that weariness is the distinguishing mark of Christians today. We work in a modern paraphrase of Matthew 11:28–29: 'Come to me, all you who are weary and burdened, and I will make you more weary. Take my causes upon you and create more self-help programmes and church initiatives and you will increase weariness for your already burdened souls.'

The virus of technique

Alongside the church's activism is another symptom related to all our endeavours. We operate with what a friend calls 'the virus of technique'. We see this in the reduction of the Christian life to self-help. We reduce reading the Bible to a technique. Seven steps, eleven steps – you take your pick. I'm not suggesting there is no merit in these approaches, but they highlight how the virus of technique always strives to find the best way. I see the same trend with prayer, or in how you can become a better spouse or parent, and so on. There's a tonne of writing on how to grow into the complete man or woman of God.

The danger is that we rely on these techniques rather than on Christ. As a young Christian, I was a sucker for the latest self-help book – the five-step process to being holy or to a more intimate relationship with Jesus. I longed for these realities, and the promise of a shortcut through a self-help strategy was irresistible. After implementing the steps, I soon became disillusioned as they failed to deliver. They fail because self-help shortcuts try to copy what God has done in someone else's life, rather than seeking him to deal with us individually in our own situation. It amazes me how, despite disillusionment, we keep falling for the next one that comes along.

The same virus of technique works on the corporate level in our various church initiatives. We see it at work as our churches get packaged so we can achieve our ends in a more streamlined way. Technique comes into its own when growing the church. Something has happened so it works by technique alone and is no longer the Spirit's business. We pursue growth through marketing, and presentation is everything. Rather than centring on Christ who is good news for sinners, it's as if we are selling the Christian life as a product to potential customers.

We can find plenty of organizations to help churches find their brand. For example, '5 Step Church Marketing Makeover': 'how you can makeover your marketing to increase the number of guests and avoid losing them through the back door'.[3] I've sat in church planting seminars that have guaranteed success if you follow the right steps. Even doing evangelism is a technique, and sharing the gospel becomes a marketing pitch.

We trust in these strategies to build our causes. When any novel idea gets trialled, it is packaged and franchised so everyone can give it a go. We have the knack for turning everything into a fast-food brand.

The corporatized church

Our activist stance, bolstered by technique, has given rise to another observable symptom. We are turning the church into a corporate enterprise. This changes the way we operate into something that mirrors a commercial business. Pastors are becoming CEOs, elders are members of governance boards, and congregants are customers. As with any business, we must compete with competitors for the market. The church has become its own consumer thing. Evangelism and church growth programmes use the latest market research to further the cause. By virtue of their size, mega churches tend to have the monopoly. This kind of corporatization makes building the church more in our hands than in Christ's.

The diagnosis

It is now time to consider the diagnosis for these symptoms. Is there a common thread, an underlying sickness, that ties all of these symptoms together?

I believe so: celebrity culture, therapeutic Christianity, activist churches, technique-driven churches and the corporatized church all share a common wellspring. Egoism accounts for them all. And

---

3 '5 Step Church Marketing Makeover', Church Brand Guide, <churchbrandguide. com/5-step-makeover>.

what is egoism? It is the cultural value set up as an ideal that revolves around humans. The word 'ego' is a synonym for 'self'. It signifies what is at the core of a human person. Call it our control centre from where everyone identifies themselves with a capital 'I'. It's our nucleus, where we use the 'I' word like no one else; 'I am English;' 'I thought about you;' 'I want the latest iPhone;' 'I did my tax return.' Each of us carries a sense of our self as someone unique. We enshrine our ego in the infamous trinity of 'Me, Myself and I'.

So that in everything humans may have the supremacy

Rémi Brague reminds us in *Curing Mad Truths* that we are living in 'The Cult of the Ego'. He writes:

> This was the title of a trilogy of novels by the late-nineteenth- and early-twentieth-century French writer Maurice Barrès. This cult has swollen into an epidemic ever since, under several names: personal development, self-fulfilment, wellness, and pursuits of that ilk.[4]

And egoism undergirds secular humanism. Its goal is this: that in everything humans may have the supremacy. Raised to the highest place, humans have appointed themselves as the new centre of reality. Without exaggeration, egoism fashions humanity as the new gods. We ground it in a self-belief brimming over with optimism at our capabilities. On a personal and individual level, it functions with the assumption that each of us has an infinite reservoir of inner resources to draw from. Given the right conditions, we can create our best self and a better world. An unshakeable trust in ourselves is the dominating ideal of our culture.

---

4   Rémi Brague, *Curing Mad Truths: Medieval Wisdom for the Modern Age* (Indiana: University of Notre Dame Press, 2019), p. 20.

We could say egoism was the original temptation the humans faced back in Genesis 3. It was Satan's first lie and his best one. He said to Adam and Eve, 'You will be like God' (v. 5). Those five words were an enticement for the first couple to transfer their trust from God to themselves. The message of Satan was, 'Hey, humans, life is about you. Follow your own path and trust your own instincts for a better version of you. So eat the forbidden fruit.'

Egoism is an ideal at odds with the Bible's teaching, which tells us that trusting ourselves is folly. God has designed us for a trust that reaches beyond our human limitations to himself. He is a reservoir of unlimited resources for us to draw on. That was true even before we fell for Satan's lie. Since the fall, the self has been corrupted. The divine verdict on humans is that we are not a reservoir of unbounded possibilities for good. Rather, the heart is deceitful above all things and desperately wicked. The super-value of egoism is at odds with the revelation of the self in the Bible. It commits our culture to its own version, leading to a massive inflation of the ego and resulting in our becoming full of ourselves.

I had an amusing experience of this on a long-haul flight to the southern hemisphere. As I settled into my economy-class seat, a flight attendant bundled a youthful man through the doors just before they closed and plonked him down next to me. He informed me that first class was his normal mode of travel. 'My office totally messed up the booking.' I expressed commiserations and wished him a pleasant flight.

As soon as the plane was in the air, he took out his laptop and, before I could blink, a naked man filled the screen. I averted my gaze in embarrassment, and was stunned when he nudged me. 'Do you know who this is?' I took a peek and, lo and behold, it was an image of the very chap next to me. He explained that he was a model who worked for an agency that got his picture in leading advertising campaigns. His job on this flight was to work over a photo before its release in a men's magazine.

When I enquired why his office didn't undertake the task, he said he trusted no one with perfecting the image of himself. And so, with a computer program designed for such things, he blew up the pixels and did a makeover, removing every blemish. For ten hours he worked on the image of himself. It was a spectacular 'all about me' experience.

As if to allay any doubts I might have concerning who he said he was, as my hosts drove me through the city, I saw an advert with his torso displayed to the world.

Egoism functions in this kind of self-aggrandizement. It makes the self fill the horizon of everything that is part of our modern culture – a self-belief that has the feel of something religious. Listen and you will hear the language of faith applied to this super-value – like a believer talking about faith in Christ. Shannon Terrell promotes it in these terms: 'Learning how to believe in yourself with un-stoppable, unshakable faith is a skill. And the good news is, it's a skill you can cultivate and develop.'[5]

'Because you're worth it'

It doesn't take great observational skills to see reflections of this super-value today. 'Believe in yourself' is the moral of the story in every Disney film and the basic message in every graduation speech. We can see egoism behind most advertising. Watch a standard commercial for any car and you'll discover the reason for buying is not about the quality of the vehicle but because of the way it will enhance your image and increase your power. It's a memo telling you how to release a better version of yourself.

Consider also some classic straplines that various brands use to convey their products:

- 'Because you're worth it' (L'Oreal);

---

5   Shannon Terrell, 'How To Believe In Yourself With Unshakable Faith', Mindvalley, 19 May 2019, <blog.mindvalley.com/how-to-believe-in-yourself>.

- 'Power to you' (a past Vodafone slogan);
- 'Just do it' (Nike).

We could extend the list to fill a chapter. Such slogans appeal to egoism's ideal – how to upgrade to a better version of you. It functions out of a positivity, the kind that is *ex nihilo* and constructed out of thin air. We see this in many bestsellers. Take the book by Jonathan Heston with the not-so-subtle title of *The Unlimited Self*.[6] There is no end to 'believe in yourself' books, and they sell because they traffic something that has great appeal. There are countless professional gurus and life coaches who peddle the same message – how to overcome your doubts by believing in yourself; how to reach your true potential. The self-belief gospel has raised its own army of preachers.

A very brief history

How did egoism become a super-value reaching such an ascendant place in our culture? It's worth noting the obvious that human selfishness is not new. Since Genesis 3, humans have been selfish, and our natural orientation is self-centred. But only recently has it become endorsed as something positive. It wasn't so long ago that we frowned upon it – even if we indulged it. What is novel in our time is how it has become lauded as a virtue. As one writer puts it, 'self-reliance is the greatest of all virtues my friend'.[7] The more you centre on you and treasure yourself, the better. Something has shifted.

We can grasp this by appreciating that every society in the ancient world centred on its gods. The prominent place given to the temples that housed them symbolized this (as we saw in chapter 1). Individuals may have been self-centred, but it was never a cultural ideal.

---

6 Jonathan Heston, *The Unlimited Self: Destroy Limiting Beliefs, Uncover Inner Greatness, and Live the Good Life* (CreateSpace Independent Publishing Platform, 2015).
7 Abhijit Naskar, *Rowdy Buddha: The First Sapiens* (CreateSpace Independent Publishing Platform, 2017, Kindle edition), Part 2, Buddhahood.

They arranged society around the gods, and humans were subservient in this arrangement. It was another world from what the egoism ideal promotes today.

It isn't easy to pinpoint when the ego revolution began. Through the seventeenth and eighteenth centuries we availed ourselves of new scientific methods and uncovered many of the 'secrets' of nature. These insights provided us with greater powers to control our lives. It was an age of unprecedented accomplishments. Take modern medicine as an example. In the premodern world, one of the pre-scribed cures for gout was this:

Take an owl and pluck it clean and open it, clean and salt it. Put it in a new pot and cover it with a stone and put it in an oven and let it stand till it be burnt. And then stamp [pound] it with boar's grease and anoint the gout therewith.[8]

The new science opened the door to medical practices based on something that worked, improving our health and prolonging our lives.

Humanism's golden age

This set off a golden age in terms of scientific progress and discovery. It may not have been a golden age for those who toiled in the factories of Europe's industrial revolution, but it did shift our trust from God to ourselves. No doubt the biggest discovery was doing life without him. When the great French scholar Pierre-Simon Laplace was questioned by Napoleon as to why he had written a huge book on the system of the world without any mention of its author, he famously replied that he had no need of that hypothesis.

And so God was displaced from the centre and the self-belief ideal grew. As this God displacement gained traction, humans became more

---

8   Nicholas Sokic, 'WTF: Medieval medicine was wacky, but it worked', Healthing: Inspiring Canadians to Live Better, 25 February 2020, <www.healthing.ca/science/ wtf-medieval-medicine-might-have-treated-deadly-bacteria>.

central to European culture, and the God revealed in the Bible became more peripheral. A large proportion of society continued to profess some kind of belief in God, but this became increasingly private.

It was in the nineteenth century that Friedrich Nietzsche pronounced that God was dead. As believers we know he continues to be the living God, but our culture has stopped believing. Belief in God shifted to self-belief. In terms of a cultural ideal, humans have made the self central.

I am describing here the rise of a movement called secular humanism. The writer Abhijit Naskar states the heart of this in his book with the provocative title *Principia Humanitas*. He writes that 'the Human Self is the only friend and savior to all humanity'.[9] If God were dead, who else could we believe in? We had only ourselves to trust, and so egoism replaced our belief in God.

When we grapple with egoism, it is important that we don't neglect the spell-binding reasons for self-belief. It has a persuasive plausibility with our accomplishments to substantiate it. In the humanist age, our exploits are on a scale never seen before: cars, aeroplanes, rockets with the capacity to launch us into space. Electricity, lasers, wireless and the worldwide web – the list of wonders extends beyond our capacity to even name them. So great is the age of humanism that one wonders if calling this super-value a 'pretension' is the correct way to label it. As something for our confidence and trust, it appears justified. The egoism ideal is vindicated, and who can challenge it? No wonder, of the four super-values, this one is king and beyond dispute.

A taxonomy of egoism

Having looked at the big idea behind egoism, it is time to do a basic taxonomy of how it works itself out in our culture. How is this ideal

9   Abhijit Naskar, *Principia Humanitas: Self is All (First Principle of Humanism)* (CreateSpace Independent Publishing Platform, 2017).

expressed? Egoism works like a two-sided coin. The one side operates with a focus on us, concentrating on generating self-belief. The other side of the coin involves us unleashing our potential into the world with an external focus. Once nurtured, our self-belief must then express itself. We shall see how this works with a pre-determined method.

The first step requires us to build up trust and confidence in ourselves. What makes this necessary is that humans have lots of self-doubt. Uncertainty of our value and worth plagues us. To overcome, we must look inward, crediting ourselves with the good that lies dormant there. Self-belief functions in a strong positivity. It's a call to affirm our nobility and splendour. You are an untapped reservoir of abilities and possibilities. The key thing is to get in touch with the better you. Nurture this 'you'; develop positive feelings about this 'you'. It's a call to confidence and trust in who and what you are, and there are enough inspirational quotes communicating this idea to sink the *Titanic*!

As soon as you trust yourself, you will know how to live.
(Johann Wolfgang von Goethe)[10]

With realization of one's own potential and self-confidence in one's ability, one can build a better world.
(Dalai Lama)[11]

Always be yourself and have faith in yourself. Do not go out and look for a successful personality and try to duplicate it.
(Bruce Lee)[12]

Love yourself first and everything else falls into line. You really have to love yourself to get anything done in this world.
(Lucille Ball)[13]

---

10 Attributed.
11 Attributed.
12 Attributed.
13 Attributed.

> Just believe in yourself. Even if you don't, pretend that you do and, at some point, you will.
> (Venus Williams)[14]

And my personal favourite:

> Always be yourself! Unless you can be Batman, then always be Batman.
> (Jayy Von Monroe)[15]

These give expression to the self-belief ideal, and there is a truth in it we should not ignore. The power of every lie is that it exists as a half-truth. The half-truth here – an important and biblical one – is that every human person has a value and preciousness beyond anything else in creation. Humans are, after all, made in the image of God – and that makes us fearfully and wonderfully made. Because of the way our Creator designed us, we have a set of remarkable capacities, each with potential for making a significant impact. So, we can affirm the truth of human potential within the egoism ideal.

However, while recognizing humanity's potential, the Bible shows us we have a dark side. Sin has caused ruination by turning us away from God and towards ourselves. Here, a significant contrast shows up. Egoism rests in an idea that humans are a reservoir of good just waiting to be released. Christianity asserts that humans are creatures of great value but corrupted. Our potential is distorted by our tendency to selfishness, and our amazing capacities give us the potential for great evil as well as great good.

This tainting includes our self-doubt, a despoiling in the form of our insecurities. Often this extends to the point of self-loathing, and from such a place it incapacitates us in terms of what we might achieve. Self-belief is egoism's way of redeeming us from our internal

---

14 Attributed.
15 Attributed.

insecurities. The Bible affirms another path. Sin has bent us so out of shape in our inner life that only Christ can help.

But culture without Christ looks elsewhere for deliverance – the intervention of the therapist. Most people cannot embrace the unqualified positivity about themselves that egoism asserts. We carry baggage from our past, hindering a belief in ourselves. Picking up negative messages from our parents and peers leaves us in shame and self-loathing. The therapist (or life coach) is the healer to untangle the negativity, releasing us to become more self-confident and 'believers in ourselves'. I say this not to decry therapy as wrong. There is much in psychology that shines a light on our destructive internal dynamics. Used well, therapy can give us tools to overcome negative thoughts and feelings. But to the extent that we seek ultimate fulfilment in self-belief, therapy can easily become a handmaiden to the egoism ideal.

Realizing our potential through the best technique

The goal of acquiring self-belief is for self-realization – to live out who we are. Once self-belief is in place, we must pursue our potential. Here is the other side of the coin of egoism. The outward expression of our self-belief is our self-actualization, which must utilize what I will call the 'tool of technique'. Technique is itself an ideal born in our thought and imagination. It is about the best way to achieve our goals. Once worked out as an ideal, we then put it into practice, and in a process of trial and error the technique is honed and refined until we discover the best way.

When I lived in L'Abri with my family, we cooked for large numbers of guests, leaving a sizable stack of dishes. Over the course of twenty-one years I developed a technique for getting through them with the greatest efficiency and the help of a few volunteers. As I abhorred the waterfall method for rinsing, the technique meant using the least amount of water while utilizing the quickest way to clean a kitchen. It also confronted me with the challenge of using 'amateur' help. How could I school them in my technique without coming across as a dishwashing tyrant?

Over time and with lots of practice, I 'perfected' my method. I came to believe I was a world-class washer of crockery and cutlery (the first step in egoism). Then I came to believe in my technique after years of putting it into practice (step two in egoism). If a market existed for a book on the best way to wash dishes, I might have written it! Sadly, the existence of dishwashers makes my expertise redundant.

We live in a culture where we reduce everything to a technique. Each is a tool enabling us to reach our potential, and an essential part of egoism. Techniques exist for relaxation, stress reduction and memory improvement. There is a 'how to' for getting the man or woman of your dreams, and how to achieve the greatest pleasure in sex. You can find plenty of techniques to attain your best level of fitness. For anyone who wants to be a world beater, there are lots of how-to options. Take the triumphant *7 Habits of Highly Effective People*, written by Steve Covey, as an example. Our love affair with technique has spawned the world of 'self-help', assisting us on the path to becoming our better self. Even though your form of the best way may conflict with another's, the key is to believe in your diet or fitness regime even when your best friend touts another.

I do not want you to misunderstand me. Technique in and of itself is not wrong – and it is a wonderful capacity given by God. We create techniques to exercise our dominion over creation. Humans have always used techniques to create new openings, leading to advancements in every field – beginning with agriculture. The difference in the 'egoism' ideal is that technique has become the focus of our trust for dominating the world.

And techniques really do dominate! We assume they have a universal application working across different cultures and locations. A church grows in one place, and we package the method for use everywhere and franchise it out. Techniques condition us to treat people and communities as things to be programmed rather than as entities with their own histories and feelings. But we use them to achieve what we think will lead to the best outcomes. That is why the humanist age has invested so much in techniques. We must become our best self without risk of failure, and to ensure this we need the reliability of a proven method. It's all about trust!

When we put together the two sides of egoism, we have a partnership of invincibility – self-belief plus technique. The potential lying dormant within us becomes self-realized when we appropriate the right tools and methods. They work, and no one should doubt what a potent combination this double-sided ideal provides. Belief in ourselves and in our techniques is the focus for our new confidence and trust. Through both, we have ascended to the prominent place and fulfilled our potential. Humans rule the world, and the apostle John's little phrase 'the pride of life' is the perfect description (1 John 2:16). Welcome to egoism's brave new world!

Egoism and the church's disordered trust

So let's apply the 'egoism' test to the contemporary church. In a typical church today, we can detect the same double arrangement of egoism. We may package it with a Christ garnish, but in substance it is identical. We seek God-therapies for self-realization and techniques for achieving our potential. Rather than looking to Christ, who gives us new life by calling us to die to self (Matt. 16:24–26), we trust our self-help methods where he is only a gloss to our achievements. Rather than the church being something he builds through his divine power, we trust our activities and programmes to get the job done. It's what we may experience when we help out with an evangelism course our church is running. The programme sets the agenda for the evening without a chance to explore the real questions people have. It is what a friend of mine experienced when he joined a church where every conversation with different church leaders revolved around what programme he might fit into. Clearly, they didn't know what to do with him!

The church's accommodation to egoism is a **disordered trust** – a trust focused on our potential and our techniques rather than on Christ. Our activism betrays where our trust lies. We are so busy that we have forgotten the true architect and builder of the church. The church is not a corporate enterprise; the church is Christ's living body. He animates us with his own life and power so the work can get done. It means the church is a people through whom Christ can bear his fruit. In the words of Francis Schaeffer, it's 'the Lord's work in the Lord's way'.[16]

One way to challenge egoism in the church is to ask some pointed questions. Is the emotional prosperity gospel at work? Has the implementation of our Christian pop psychologies over the past decades made us more like Jesus? Are Christians today more spiritually robust for colluding with the new religious self-improvement strategies? The reality seems to show a negative impact on the quality of our spiritual life. We can ask other challenging questions of our evangelical activism. In the post-war period, what has all this activity achieved? Has the church grown by producing in believers a greater likeness to Jesus? Have we seen our culture change for the better because of our labours? Are we making inroads in our gospel work with sceptics? These are the questions we must face.

While levelling this indictment against a self-centred church, it is important to emphasize again that, within the Christian understanding, the self is important. Equated with personhood – what the Bible calls the heart – selfhood is the jewel of creation. While stressing this, the Bible also asserts that God never intended us to be the centre. He designed us to be outward-facing. We exist not for ourselves but for others, and he intended our outward-directedness

---

16 Chapter title from Francis A. Schaeffer, *No Little People* (Wheaton, Ill.: Crossway, 2003).

to be for Christ. Living for Christ, we become more ourselves when the focus is on him.

The Bible teaches that Jesus Christ is both our centre and our sufficiency. For that reason, he alone must be the focus of our trust and confidence. Overlooking him shifts the focus of our dependence onto ourselves. With self at the centre, our ego has filled the temple. We have reformatted the church into something after our image. It is not about Christ, but about us. Our inflated view of ourselves has led to a diminished view of the Lord Jesus.

One could call this the 'Ichabod phenomenon', reflecting an incident recorded in 1 Samuel 4 when a neighbouring state captured the ark of the covenant. Ichabod was the name given to a child born on that fateful day and is the Hebrew word meaning, 'Where is the glory?' It acknowledges that the divine glory that once filled the temple had departed. With the self now filling the temple that Christ once inhabited, we are in our own Ichabod moment.

The treatment – remembering who Jesus is

The treatment for and inoculation against this super-value will only come through recovering how beautiful, powerful and glorious Jesus is. But what does the Bible mean by 'glory'? Here is a concept so rich and profound it is hard to grasp. At its core is the reality of *weightiness*. It carries the idea of substantiality, something so real that everything else appears as a lightness. When humans meet Christ as he is, they meet One who is so solid they experience the weight in a way that is life-changing. The Jewish writers of the Old Testament used the Hebrew word *kabod* to describe this heaviness of glory.

Christ's glory means he is the Absolute Real – he has an *is*-ness that is total. He is as real as real can be. It is not possible for him to become more real or less real. In fact, everything else is measured against the fullness of his being. He is the only one who can say 'I AM', identifying himself as the one God who revealed himself by this name to Moses in the burning bush (Exod. 3:14; John 8:58). He needs no reference point except his own ultimate *being*.

He alone is the self-existing One and there is no adequate reference point for him in this world. Isaiah gives expression to this:

All the nations are as nothing before him,
they are accounted by him as less than nothing
and emptiness.
To whom then will you liken God,
or what likeness compare with him?
(Isa. 40:17–18 esv uk)

Human beings, by contrast, lack this self-sufficiency. We do not have the weightiness necessary for autonomous self-expression. We are not internal reservoirs of unlimited potential. No human on his or her own can say 'I am'. And that makes us derivative. We can imagine it like a mould – human beings are derivative representations (like coins) of the original, absolute source (the mould). Christ can express himself without reference to anything or anyone else. We can't. But when we look to Christ, we receive from him an identity that is solid and unshakeable, a gift that doesn't depend on our activity or achievement.

Christ's glory includes his power

The glory of Christ includes his divine power. This is so great that humans struggle to even conceive of it, and it blows our minds when we try. We know something of the power inherent in our universe on both the macro and the micro level. An average cumulonimbus cloud – the kind that produces thunder and lightning – contains as much energy as ten Hiroshima-sized atomic bombs. The power of the One who made this universe surpasses all the combined energy and potency of his creation. Jesus' power is greater than the roaring fire of all the stars of all the countless galaxies.

Here is a vision of Christ *Pantocrator* – Jesus Almighty and All-powerful. If this is true, not even the dominant power of humans in the Secular Age can compare with him. The wonder of being his church is that it inaugurated us into this glorious power. As Jesus reminded us in the Great Commission, 'All authority in heaven and on earth has been given to me' (Matt. 28:18). Here is the One who fills our temple, and to see him like that relativizes any self-aggrandizement we may think we have. It's a portrait of One who has a grandeur that puts us in perspective, revealing our limitations. It is a revelation that unshackles us from our inflated egos and humbles us. It becomes an unselfing – we realize we are not the centre.

To pass through this experience does not demean us as his people. It is an essential part of making the best version of us. This version functions out of a trust that puts us in our proper place – the creature before our Almighty Creator. Only through his power can we accomplish anything worthwhile and lasting. The place where we must be is a church where Christ is central. We must restore him to his proper place in the temple.

Christ's glory includes his beauty and goodness

Today, power tends to be viewed with suspicion because it so often becomes ugly in human hands. But the power Jesus wields is good and beautiful, and to see him in his glory we must include this. When Jesus' people appreciate his glory, which combines power, goodness and beauty, they can only break out in spontaneous praise. The Catholic Encyclopedia tells us that Augustine used a Latin phrase reflecting glory as 'brilliant celebrity with praise'.[17] How apt for a culture that orders itself around the life of celebrities! A-list, B-list and an endless supply of magazines and websites so we can see the glory of these people.

---

17 'Glory', Catholic Online, <www.catholic.org/encyclopedia/view.php?id=5201>.

Well, when the glory of the Lord is revealed, every cult of celebrity in our world withers away. When the true, brilliant celebrity appears, all those to whom we have given this accolade will appear as nothing. They, like us, will be naked before the One who is fullness itself. And that includes our church celebrities!

Because of Christ's 'brilliant celebrity with praise', no superlative will do for describing him. We moderns love to use hyperbole; we inflate language to make a point, especially when it concerns praise of the self. I remember watching a group of people play volleyball in an English garden, and one player made an impressive dive to rescue the errant ball. His success prompted a classic hyperbole from the chap standing beside me, who turned and exclaimed, 'Freakin' awesome!' It struck me with incongruity. This phrase seems to have mounted the Everest of hyperbole – was there anything that could exceed 'freakin' awesome' in terms of praise?

I realized, if we offer such phrases to humans, we have little left to say when we encounter the weightiness and glory of the One who is at the centre of everything. But then again, when we encounter the true weight of glory, we will have reached the end of language itself. There will be no words to adequately describe this reality. Christ's glory far surpasses everything in this world and, for all the abilities humans have, is far weightier. It is the task of the church to live for the Christ who bears this weight of glory.

Worthy of our full confidence and trust

Only in recovering Christ's glory can we be cured of our dis-ordered trust. In words of unmistakable clarity, he says to his church that 'apart from me you can do nothing' (John 15:5). That means that what we attempt on our own without a trust directed towards him is not his work. Only he can achieve the self-improvement that matters – the kind that leads to the distinctiveness that marks the people of God. Only he can build his church with a life and spiritual vitality that changes the world. Again, with a clarity no one can misunderstand, he has given us an assurance that 'I will build my church' (Matt. 16:18). It really is his job.

Because of his divine glory, he is the measure of all possibility and potential – and worthy of our trust for the work he calls us to do. As alluring as the commitments of egoism are, the church must recover an unshakeable trust in Christ and his supreme glory. As seductive as egoism is, as invincible its dual commitment to self-belief and technique, it does not compare with Christ in his divine glory. We need to recover a vision of him comparable to the One presented in Isaiah 40:

> 'Here is your God!'
> See, the Sovereign LORD comes with power,
>   and he rules with a mighty arm . . .
>
> Who has measured the waters in the hollow of his hand,
>   or with the breadth of his hand marked off the heavens?
> Who has held the dust of the earth in a basket,
>   or weighed the mountains on the scales
>   and the hills in a balance? . . .
>
> 'To whom will you compare me?
>   Or who is my equal?' says the Holy One.
> Lift up your eyes and look to the heavens:
>   who created all these?
> He who brings out the starry host one by one
>   and calls forth each of them by name.
> Because of his great power and mighty strength,
>   not one of them is missing.
> (Isa. 40:9–10, 12, 25–26)

For people like Laura to find a way through their confusion as to who and what church is for, this is the Jesus they need. The church is about an unshakeable trust in this glorious person. He alone has what it takes to improve us and make us new. He alone has the power to build a church after his image, one that stands out and doesn't blend in with commitments of egoism. When our trust focuses on him, we no longer work from an activist stance but from a place of rest. And he invites us to work for his wonderful cause in this world on the basis of his Almighty power. As we are reminded in Zechariah 4:6, '"Not by [our] might nor by [our] power, but by my Spirit," says the LORD Almighty.'

Chapter summary

*Egoism is a culture value that exalts humans to the highest place with a self-belief that we have within ourselves what it takes to realize our true potential and, with the right technique, to manufacture a better world. The contemporary church has accommodated with a **disordered trust** that believes in the therapeutic as the means to our wholeness, and in the virus of technique to build our causes. These commitments have only exhausted us. To overcome this aspect of our worldliness, we must recover the knowledge of Christ in his sovereign and almighty power and place our trust in him alone.*

Questions

- If you're part of a church, what impressions might complete outsiders receive if they were to show up? If you're not part of a church, what have your impressions of churches been?
- Are you one of the wearied – and why?
- Where does a disordered trust show itself in your life and church?
- If your church has stopped praying, do you think that would make any difference to how the programmes work?
- What might church be like if awe at Christ's power and beauty really shaped its culture?

Further reading

Christopher Lasch, *The Culture of Narcissism: American Life in an Age of Diminishing Expectations* (New York; London: W. W. Norton & Co., 1991).

Ross Douthat, *Bad Religion: How We Became a Nation of Heretics* (New York: Simon & Schuster, 2012).

Jacques Ellul, *The Technological Society* (New York: Vintage Books, 1964).

Carl R. Trueman, *The Rise and Triumph of the Modern Self: Cultural Amnesia, Expressive Individualism, and the Road to Sexual Revolution* (Wheaton, Ill.: Crossway, 2020).

4

Naturalism: seeing is believing

It's not what you look at that matters, it's what you see.
(Henry David Thoreau)[1]

Ethan was representative of many who came to L'Abri in a crisis. For him it circled around the plausibility of what he believed. His issue wasn't, 'Is Christianity true?' but, 'Is Christianity real?' Like so many, he was experiencing a chronic loss of spiritual reality. You could also call it a crisis of meaning.

The presenting problem for Ethan was his nagging feeling that prayer didn't really change anything. As a conscientious Christian he had attempted to overcome this by keeping his prayers as vague as possible, not asking for anything specific to avoid the risk of disappointment. He was also smart enough to discern that this was a dodge.

Ethan had noticed, too, how prayer in his church was an afterthought, calling on God to bless something they had already rationalized and planned. He could see the incongruence between what he and his church believed and how it actually worked itself out. There was a clear hunger for something deeper and more in line with the Bible's revelation of the supernatural realm, but this seemed beyond his grasp. A deficit of experience brought Ethan to the brink of giving up his faith.

---

1 Henry David Thoreau, *Walden: 'It's Not What You Look at That Matters, It's What You See'* (UK: Scope Publishing, 2015).

Symptoms of a disorder

Tragically, another aspect of our present worldliness is that the church is losing the reality of the supernatural. I wonder if you've been to one of those churches that doesn't feel particularly different from a coffee shop. Neutral décor and mediocre coffee in a hired school hall or a converted warehouse. Mirroring shopping centres and warehouses, it all looks so flattened and horizontal – demonstrating the plane on which we are operating. Even beyond the practical constraints of finding a suitable venue to meet in, there often seems to be no attempt to evoke any sense of transcendence. Living as though planet Earth is the complete package dominates the horizons of our vision.

Part of our current forgetfulness is how to live the reality of a faith that practically engages with the supernatural and all that we have in Christ. In a quite literal way, this fits the meaning of being worldly. Although on Sundays we might celebrate Jesus and his amazing miracles, our day-to-day view of reality so easily forgets that 'in him we live and move and have our being' (Acts 17:28).

Making sense of events spiritually

One discernible symptom of this loss of spiritual reality is how we decipher events. How do you view matters when things go wrong? Perhaps you put it down to bad luck. Or maybe you worry that God is punishing you. But when we have a supernatural perspective, we know both that Christ is in control and that he's working all things together for our good, even if it's hard to see this from our limited perspective.

Scripture encourages us to understand everything that happens through the grid of Providence. That is the theological term for the reality that in Christ 'all things hold together' (Col. 1:17). He has the universe in his hands, and what is significant about these hands is that they are safe. As history works itself out, with all its twists and turns, our viewpoint allows us to assert that 'all shall be well and thou shalt see for thyself that all manner of things shall be well', as Julian of Norwich put it.[2] Why? Because history – including every detail of our personal histories – is under the oversight of Christ. We see this theme running through the Bible, from Joseph's recognition that what his brothers had intended for evil in selling him into slavery, God had intended for good (Gen. 50:20), to Jesus' reassurance that not even a sparrow falls apart from the Father (Matt. 10:29), to Paul's reminder to us that God works all things together for the good of those who love him (Rom. 8:28). Everything will end up where he has determined.

We can feel confident that everything is going to be alright because we have a vision of reality that sees further. Here is what enables followers of Jesus to keep going even when the times are tough. Providence allows us to trace the good hand of Christ in the details of our existence. When spiritual realities become dim, so does this insight. Becoming earthbound in our outlook, we lose the ability to suffer well. Many Christians become disillusioned when subjected to suffering, without being provided with the spiritual realities needed to experience God in their sufferings.

Living in the hope of Christ's return

Our sense of spiritual unreality affects not only how we understand the present, but also our view of the future. A common symptom is that we forget to live in the light of Christ's second coming. As Paul put it, Christians are those who 'wait for the blessed hope – the appearing of the glory of our great God and Saviour, Jesus Christ' (Titus 2:13). The Bible is clear that we are to live in constant expectation of his return. That is why through the ages Christians have lived with the word *Maranatha* on their lips – 'O Lord, come!' This is history's last grand miracle – the second advent of Christ. He is

---

2 Julian of Norwich, *Love's Trinity: A Companion to Julian of Norwich* (Minnesota: Liturgical Press, 2009), p. 249.

going to break into history in the most dramatic form to finish the work he began.

Here is what makes up the greatest hope of the Christian: Jesus is the end of history and the last man. In the framework of human history, this will be the greatest of supernatural events. Jesus will raise the dead to life at the resurrection, and death will be destroyed (1 Cor. 15:20–28); 'creation itself will be liberated from its bondage to decay' (Rom. 8:21), so that those who have trusted Jesus will live with him for ever in the new creation (Rev. 21:1–4). This is a world away from the prevailing scientific view of the future, with everything running down into death and decay: the future extinction of humanity, absorption of the Earth by the Sun, and the eventual end of the universe.

A gradual fading-out or a dramatic breaking-in? The hope of the believer reaches to the latter. We are meant to be gripped by this. Everything about our life is to be governed by this insight. This is what the Christian is waiting for – preparing for the greatest event of all time. Of late, this expectation has diminished and almost disappeared from the horizon of the church's vision. When was the last time you heard a sermon about Christ's return? You could attend church for a year and not once hear that this is what we hope for – another sign that we are living in flatlands. But when we grasp this truth, then we live in hope, knowing that God is at work redeeming the world, and we don't succumb to impatience and disillusionment, because we know it will only come to full fruition when Jesus returns.

The pragmatic church

Another sign of a disorder is our more pragmatic approach to everything in the church. Pragmatism operates with a practical reason that prioritizes what works. This is closely connected to the obsession with 'technique' that we looked at in the previous chapter as a symptom of Egoism, but, as we'll uncover shortly, there's another super-value at work here. We are beguiled by what we can test and measure. We stake our success on measurable outcomes. We have a survey for pretty much everything, which is the epistemic proof of our corporate life and its success. This treats reality as something quantifiable, and our job is to provide this through numbers. Service attendances up 12% and our divorce rate down 3% – so all in all a tremendous year. The numbers we crunch are then used to create our strategic goals for making things better.

Where numbers might disclose one aspect of reality, they fall short with the fullness of spiritual reality. Try reducing 'becoming like Christ' to a measurable outcome! Our obsession with numbers and outcomes shows the loss of a broader horizon.

If your church escapes this kind of crass pragmatism, you might see it in other ways. A discerning friend told me how most sermons he heard were naturalistic in their application. A Sunday service might begin well enough with the call to worship and a reminder of the supernatural realities of our faith. But come the moment of application for life, it always defaulted to one of what he called the 'five mores'. Attend *more*, Evangelize *more*, Read your Bible *more*, Pray *more* and Give *more*. One could hear such solicitations for months and never be struck by the deeper reality of the supernatural. My wife and I use the acronym 'E. A.' to describe this. This stands for 'evangelical advice' and 'easy answers'.

Losing wonder

We might also see the symptoms in a rationalistic approach to the faith. Many churches are shackled by a view of the Bible as a mine to be quarried for theological facts. They equate a solid faith with one that has intellectual mastery of all the finer points of theology. A sense of wonder has all but disappeared. Whether someone's life is filled with the goodness and grace of Jesus is a question that fades into the background. As the scientific outlook removes mystery and has an observable proof for everything, so the church has followed suit by domesticating the faith. We have developed a resistance to the unknown and the inscrutable is taboo. We even apply this to God himself.

A friend of mine became a Christian because the person who evangelized him professed a God beyond figuring out. When my friend asked why God created the world, the reply was a simple, 'I don't know.' In this answer, he acknowledged that he was dealing with a being greater than his intellect. This led him to bow before a God superior to nature and beyond the reach of science. We have domesticated him today. We shrink him to someone we think we can 'get'. Our churches seem starved of wonder, and this is symptomatic of a deeper malaise, even among so-called 'sound' churches.

The diagnosis

Let's gather together the symptoms: a nagging sense of spiritual unreality, 'flattened' church that mirrors the world around it, a way of looking at our present and future that forgets Jesus, pragmatism and an obsession with what's measurable, and a loss of wonder.

The super-value making sense of all these symptoms is naturalism. And what is this mega ideal? It is a view of reality that sees matter as the source of all things. Everything has an explanation in physics and biology. Julian Huxley was a famous scientist who championed naturalism in the twentieth century. He proclaimed, 'There is no separate supernatural realm: all phenomena are part of one natural process of evolution.'[3]

Such a viewpoint also applies to history, and that means there are no miracles. The incarnation couldn't have happened, giving a new spin to the birth of Jesus in Bethlehem. With no miracles, Pentecost didn't happen, meaning there was no pouring out of the Holy Spirit as the breath of God for creating his church. No miracles also means

---

3   Julian Huxley, *Evolutionary Humanism* and *Essays of a Humanist* (United Kingdom: Rationalist Press Association Limited, 1964), p. 134.

our future resurrection inaugurated by Christ's second coming is a futile hope.

This viewpoint is well expressed in the lyrics of 'Imagine' by John Lennon: there is no heaven but only sky above our heads. That's not so hard to imagine because this is the status quo of how everyone lives today.

The poet T. S. Eliot thought there was no way of avoiding the dilemma of being either a naturalist or a supernaturalist.[4] A key tenet of Christianity is its affirmation of the supernatural. What we believe depends on the reality of God's supernatural revelation. Take our starting point – the existence of a Triune God. Week by week, Christians gather to gaze with the eye of faith on the One who transcends nature. He has the kind of being that is awesome and beyond measure. As his worshippers, we know there is more to the world than what our sensory perceptions can access, and that allows us to believe in certainties that have no direct empirical proof to warrant them. As supernaturalists we recognize much that exists beyond the remit of scientific validation. Indeed, all the fundamentals of Christian belief stem from something that is not reducible to nature. God's creation of the universe *ex nihilo* (out of nothing), the virgin birth of Jesus Christ, his resurrection from the dead and the Holy Spirit's miracle of new birth in us: all these and more are rooted in realities nature cannot account for.

Recovering spiritual reality

It was not wrong for Ethan to expect to experience spiritual reality because Christians are called to live in two orders of experience. First-order experience relates to what is immediate to our senses. God has designed us for a rich involvement in a world engaging sight, sound, taste, smell and touch. After a long and dreary winter, the sun came out and my wife and I headed for the seaside. Sitting in my deckchair

---

4   T. S. Eliot, *Selected Essays* (Boston: Houghton Mifflin Harcourt, 2014), p. 397.

with the rays caressing my face and a cold beer in my hand, I listened to the sea washing up on the shore and embraced first-order experience. As I looked out on the ocean, it filled up my senses.

Second-order experience is different. Here we perceive and encounter through the eye of faith. Between the realm of the natural and the supernatural is a veil or cloud. To see through to this realm, we require what Paul calls 'the eyes of your heart' (Eph. 1:18). He prays for these eyes to be opened so we can perceive what is there. It's a seeing that goes deeper, reaching to the 'supernatural'. Without this crucial second sight, Christianity loses its vitality, and we can drift into forgetfulness.

A vivid example of this is when Elisha and his servant woke up early one morning to discover a hostile mob intent on doing them harm. 2 Kings 6:15–17 records it like this:

> When the servant of the man of God got up and went out early the next morning, an army with horses and chariots had surrounded the city. 'Oh no, my lord! What shall we do?' the servant asked.
>
> 'Don't be afraid,' the prophet answered. 'Those who are with us are more than those who are with them.'
>
> And Elisha prayed, 'Open his eyes, LORD, so that he may see.' Then the LORD opened the servant's eyes, and he looked and saw the hills full of horses and chariots of fire all around Elisha.

As believers, Christ calls us moment by moment to live in the reality of this unseen realm – to see with the eyes of faith. This allows us to probe further into the depths of reality and see more than the physical eye can.

It is important to clarify that second-order experience should never be a flight from the actual world. The supernatural is part of created reality, a dimension that deepens our appreciation of the natural rather than separating us from it. Seeing with the eyes of the heart is seeing the world as *God's* world, created by him full of meaning and purpose, to be received with thanksgiving.

Christians sometimes get this wrong and think second-order experience is a mystical leap into another universe. In his writing, Francis Schaeffer raised his concern about the new 'super spirituality'[5] – a bewildering notion as if we live in two universes. God has designed things so the two orders of experience are integrated. They are not in conflict because they belong to one reality. To live in the supernatural is not to engage something far off. Its reality is always near and at hand. This insight must grip us at all times. To enjoy a moment on the beach is to live in the supernatural. A simple heartfelt thank you to Christ for the sun and cold beer integrated me into both first- and second-order experience.

I love the way G. K. Chesterton understood the integration of both:

> Shall I tell you the secret of the whole world? It is that we have only known the back of the world. We see everything from behind, and it looks brutal. That is not a tree, but the back of a tree. That is not a cloud, but the back of a cloud. Cannot you see that everything is stooping and hiding a face? If we could only get round in front.[6]

As things are at the moment, we can't get round to the front for a direct look. 'We live by faith, not by sight' (2 Cor. 5:7). Faith, however, is still a viewpoint integrating us into the reality of what's on the other side.

The Holy Spirit equips all believers for second-order experience. With the eye of faith, we can be certain of what we cannot see. This

5 Francis A. Schaeffer, *The Complete Works of Francis A. Schaeffer: A Christian View of Spirituality* (Wheaton: Crossway Books, 1985), introduction to Volume 3: Book Three.
6 G. K. Chesterton, *The Man Who was Thursday* (San Francisco: Ignatius, 1999), p. 247.

is not an irrational leap but the quiet confidence of a truth that science cannot validate. Paul uses the language of a heavenly inheritance to describe what we have here. We are blessed right now 'with every spiritual blessing in Christ' (Eph. 1:3). We are always in the love of a Father who has set his affection on us. By faith we have a way of approach that allows us to 'enter' these great realities. They may be unseen, but to the eye of faith they are real. Because of this we see further than the physical eye. We have a spiritual vision giving us deep insight into the fullness of reality. And this goes further than the theoretical. And that's what spiritual wisdom is – insight into the real.

Functional naturalists

I believe the life of the church today is significantly reduced to first-order experience. We live more according to the coordinates of the seen, so the unseen fades out. When I say we are earthbound, I mean that our life is tied to the here and now. John Lennon asked us in 'Imagine' to picture a world where everyone lives for today – well, that's us, all about immediacy. This has produced the loss of spiritual reality. For many who struggle with the Christian faith, it is this that brings them to the brink. They long to be immersed in something real, and a shortfall on this side results in large numbers abandoning the faith.

Losing spiritual reality leads to a serious impoverishment in how we live out the faith. Our life as Christians is meant to be a constant faith response to the great supernatural realities. That means the quality of our faith is the degree to which these realities are real. When the supernatural fades into the background, there will be an impact on our living and practice.

One obvious implication will be on our praying. Prayer is a declaration of our dependence – one that reaches to the supernatural for help. When we are radical supernaturalists, we know that without Christ and his Spirit we can do nothing. When second sight fails us, we perceive how things work in much the same way as a naturalist.

We become what you might call 'functional naturalists'. Intercession becomes unnatural and we commit to a world that is only cause and effect. Our insight cannot pierce through to the unseen, and that makes it harder to trust that God really intervenes because we pray.

In 1936, Albert Einstein responded to a child who wrote and asked if scientists pray. He replied:

> Scientific research is based on the idea that everything that takes place is determined by laws of nature, and therefore this holds for the action of people. For this reason, a research scientist will hardly be inclined to believe that events could be influenced by a prayer, i.e. by a wish addressed to a Super-natural Being.[7]

Living within the fullness of reality gives the believer a different perspective. God can and does intervene in the affairs of this world in answer to our petitions. While affirming this, we should be careful not to reduce God to a wish-granting machine. Prayer is first of all communication, the kind that is key to all relationships. We have no warrant to expect an automatic 'yes' to everything we ask for. Part of the trust we exercise in our praying is that he knows what's best for us. But neither should we stop asking or stop expecting him to answer prayer just because a response isn't clear and obvious.

In atoms all things hold together

We can see naturalism as a worldview everywhere. Its underlying assumptions are taken for granted and not even questioned any more. Whether in a science class or a wildlife documentary, this outlook rules. The material realm is the great absolute – the sum of everything with nothing left out. So, rather than 'in [Christ] all things hold together' (Col. 1:17), it believes that 'in atoms all things

---

7   Helen Dukas and Banesh Hoffman (eds), *Albert Einstein, The Human Side: Glimpses from His Archives* (Princeton: Princeton University Press, 2013), p. 32.

hold together'. That means naturalism is a viewpoint committed to this world being all there is.

What is excluded from this vision is God. In his book, *The Experience of God*, David Bentley Hart expresses it like this:

> The reason the very concept of God has become at once so impoverished, so thoroughly mythical, and ultimately so incredible for so many modern persons is not because of all the interesting things we have learned over the past few centuries, but because of all the vital things we have forgotten.[8]

It is important to appreciate that atheism is a perspective flowing from the naturalist outlook. G. K. Chesterton once quipped that 'if there were no God, there would be no atheists'.[9] He is revealing a cosmic irony. Here's a viewpoint grounded in a negative – in what doesn't exist. Atheism is a stance arising as a hostile reaction to God. It's a viewpoint that depends on God! Despite the ironies, many have signed up. God is only a human invention – a prop for the weak-minded. Naturalism is a call to modern people to come of age and outgrow our God fantasies. It assures us this will be no loss but new freedom. Greg Graffin writes, 'Naturalism teaches one of the most important things in this world. There is only this life, so live wonderfully and meaningfully.'[10] Here we see the naturalist viewpoint presented with such plausibility.

A way of seeing

Naturalism likes to show its hand today by giving Christianity (and all religions) a thrashing. It has its prophets – figures like Richard Dawkins

---

8   David Bentley Hart, *The Experience of God: Being, Consciousness, Bliss* (New Haven: Yale University Press, 2013), p. 192.

9   G. K. Chesterton, 'Where All Roads Lead' (essay published in *Blackfriars* Magazine, 1922), <www.ecatholic2000.com/cts/untitled-711.shtml>.

10 Cited in Preston Jones (ed.), *Is Belief in God Good, Bad or Irrelevant? A Professor and a Punk Rocker Discuss Science, Religion, Naturalism and Christianity* (USA: IVP, 2006), p. 39.

and Sam Harris – whose job is to debunk the superstitions and delusions of the faith. Unlike egoism as a positive endorsement of human potential, naturalism expresses itself through scorn of the old way of seeing things. It presents Christianity as something implausible and absurd and therefore to be mocked. Take the famous Hitchens 3:16 (as proposed by the late Christopher Hitchens): 'For God so loved the world, that he gave his only begotten Son, that whosoever believeth in him will believeth in anything.'[11] Today, many may baulk at this variety of strident atheism, but the naturalistic assumptions they herald are still widely shared.

Back in chapter 2 we looked at how a cultural ideal becomes 'taken for granted', getting embedded in our way of seeing things. The power of an ideal is that this happens inadvertently. Talk to secular people and the majority could not spell out the finer points of philosophical naturalism. They probably wouldn't set out to disprove God in the light of science and reason. Indeed, many today are open to new forms of spirituality. But in the way they engage with the world they are full-blooded naturalists. My concern in this chapter is how naturalism affects our vision. We must give special consideration to the 'view' element of this world*view*. Here we touch on the most significant thing. Big ideas affect how we see, because we project our viewpoints on to the world.

So how does this work? Our Creator has endowed us with this remarkable capacity to mind the world. We have mental faculties giving us the ability to 'know'. Like a horse moving over a field grazing for grass, humans graze the world for knowledge. However, in our grazing we are not neutral, and what we come to know will depend on what we've already learned. We recognize something in the world we already believe.

An example of this is the placebo effect. If we go to the doctor and are given tablets to cure our illness, we believe the tablets will do the

11 '99 Inspirational Quotes from Christopher Hitchens That Everyone Can Agree On', The Famous People, <https://quotes.thefamouspeople.com/christopher-hitchens-3719.php>.

trick. We base this on a prior belief that doctors don't lie and tablets do what it says on the bottle. Such is the power of this knowledge that people get better even though the tablets were smarties! Another way to understand it is through appreciating that everyone works with a presupposition. We bring a preconceived vision to our knowledge pursuits, and this determines how we view things.

Naturalism is the prevailing preconception forming the outlook of humans today. It is the viewpoint that only matter matters. Naturalists exclude everything that is not in the realm of matter as illusionary. In his book *Unspirituality: Permission to be Human*, the writer Christopher Loren puts it like this: 'Let me make this radiantly clear – if you believe in spirits and the metaphysical world, your biology will create the illusion that these things are real.'[12] This statement conveniently ignores the possibility of a naturalist viewpoint creating illusions. Neuroscience has helped us appreciate how the brain is shaped by the world outside our heads. What we behold really does affect our biology. If naturalists see only matter, then their biology will create the illusion that this is everything. Welcome to the vision of the Secular Age!

A very brief history

Naturalism as a way of seeing things grew out of the modern scientific consensus. This began within a Christian way of viewing the world. A key figure in the seventeenth-century scientific revolution was Johann Kepler. He formulated the laws of planetary motion. For him, research was thinking God's thoughts after him. A well-ordered world marked by design is what we would expect from the God revealed in the Bible. We can surely find such an order in the physical realm. So, let's examine nature and figure out how it works.

---

12 Christopher Loren, *Unspirituality: Permission to be Human* (Createspace Independent Publishing Platform, 2016, Kindle edition).

This kind of enquiry delivered some wonderful insights. Nature is not enchanted with magic and miracles. Instead, it is a theatre of wonders known by probing its operation. Scientists like William Harvey explored the marvels of the human body, describing how the heart circulates blood to the brain and the rest of our anatomy. This kind of experimental science is known as the empirical method. Stressing the importance of observation, it looks for hard evidence that validates a conclusion.

As our discoveries of the natural world grew, the new science began to lose sight of the Creator. Led by the empirical method, we took an unnecessary leap of logic, that reality is only what we can observe. Like a microscope, empiricism is a wonderful tool. It allows us to zoom in on material realities effectively. But it's as if, having discovered the microscope, we collectively decided that only what we can see through its lens is real. We discarded as invalid the knowledge that comes from other methods and sources, ones that aren't exclusively directed to the material world.

As the supernatural does not submit to the empirical, the new science set a process in motion, raising doubts about whether it existed. With no direct proof, maybe it belongs to myth. Philosophers questioned the validity of miracles, opening the floodgates to an inference that the supernatural exists only in our imagination. We can reflect it in our conjured worlds of fantasy, like *Game of Thrones*. But no way does it belong to the real world.

In the early stages, most Europeans continued to root their identity in religion. There wasn't an outright rejection of God's existence. It was more a case of the supernatural becoming privatized and something a leap of blind faith was needed for.

It was only in the twentieth century that atheism won out. This was the logical extension of the insight that nature is the sum total of everything. It completed the radical overturning of how we had perceived things for millennia. It was also a convenient 'ideal' for disposing of God. What better way to kill him off than with the so-called scientific 'proof' that nothing exists beyond nature?

Such a vision of the world makes science the only credible knowledge provider. This is where 'scientism' comes in as another ideal. As a handmaiden to naturalism, it purports that science alone gives plausible understanding. Only science holds the key to truth. What is presently beyond our knowledge is only a matter of incomplete data. Why is the universe expanding? We don't know – even though we've coined the term 'dark energy' to get at it. But not to worry, we'll get an explanation, eventually! How does human consciousness work? Again, we don't know, but with Artificial Intelligence we may replicate it. Scientism works with the assumption that anything unknown has the possibility to become known as we continue to probe. There is no genuine mystery, but only insufficient knowledge.

No one should doubt the marvel of the scientific method – it is a wonderful tool for minding the world and uncovering many of its secrets. But for Christians, its false claims shouldn't take us in. To believe that nothing exists beyond the remit of science is a hubristic outlook. That doesn't mean that we must resort to a 'God of the gaps' to fill in what science can't explain. What the supernaturalist viewpoint asserts is that reality in its fullness cannot be reduced to a scientific viewpoint. Ironically, this includes the reality of our thinking about reality. As C. S. Lewis puts it:

> The naturalists have been engaged in thinking about Nature. They have not attended to the fact that they were thinking. The moment one attends to this it is obvious that one's own thinking cannot be merely a natural event, and that therefore something other than Nature exists.[13]

The naturalists' outlook is well described in John's little phrase, 'the lust of the eyes' (1 John 2:16). If science can subdue everything, then

---

13 C. S. Lewis, *Miracles* (London: Macmillan, 1953), p. 51.

our eyes have potential to see everything. Scientism lusts after complete knowledge. We reduce it all to what we observe and test. Such an approach to knowing the world comes with an assurance that we are part of something that isn't based on fairy tales. This is our enlightenment – we can see through former superstitions and view things based on observable facts. To see nature is to perceive the whole. What we have here is a worldview of the unconcealed. What makes up the real is what we have access to. There is nothing in reality that is not open to verification and proof. Unless we can validate something with evidence, there is no basis for believing. Therefore, if I am to believe, you must show me the data and give me the numbers! If the material realm is everything, it must be measurable and quantifiable. What can't be verified is written off as fiction.

The flattening of the world

If humans are to take control, this kind of reduction is necessary. Scientism does this by removing the realm of the supernatural. It flattens everything into its way of seeing, leading to the great disenchantment of the Secular Age. To accomplish this, it strips out what cannot be accounted for. On the origins of the universe, it strips out the direct input of a personal Creator. On what it means to be a human person, it strips out our spirit life. In history's meaning, it strips out the Lord of history who steers all things to his appointed end. No longer is it purposeful but just one fact following another. It even carves out the staggering problem of evil by reducing it to genetic disorder or a misfiring of the neurons. Its reductive insight becomes flat and one-dimensional.

Christians have every reason to affirm what science can do. Its breadth is astonishing! We also have excellent grounds for showing its limits. There are plenty of truths science cannot access. It may grant us insight into what belongs to nature, but its powers are not omniscient. There is plenty it cannot resolve, matters for which there is no proof. Here is why the 'flattening' of scientism takes away more than we bargain for. Science cannot determine human rights or prove what they should be. Neither can it offer anything that calls for an aesthetic judgment. Whether Shakespeare had a better command of language than the writer of an airport novel is not for science to say. If science is limited for something like the arts, what can it offer on the matter of the Trinity and the incarnation?

How the naturalists' vision works

Today, naturalism has a stronghold on how we 'mind' the world. It has created the flattening of the reality we live in. Nature fills the horizon of how we see things so nothing else is real and all reference points for a realm beyond the material are removed. The reality of the supernatural is implausible and consigned to imaginary works of novels and films. You can't take it seriously as part of the actual world. As a result, we conceptualize life in a materialist framework. It conditions us to see the world like this.

G. K. Chesterton was getting at this when he wrote, 'The traveller sees what he sees. The tripper sees what he has come to see.'[14] With nature, we are not travellers willing to depart from the beaten track with an openness to something serendipitous. No, we are like tourists in Rome herded along the same paths and taking the same photos on our smartphones. It's what we have come to see, and no one questions the familiar sites – nature is everything. And as we will come to understand, our viewpoint in the church is flattened by this naturalism, even while we try to maintain our belief in the supernatural.

The disenchantment of death

The naturalist vision has also affected how we deal with death. Here is another great disenchantment of our age. If you want to figure out

---

14 G. K. Chesterton, *Autobiography* (Kiribati: Hutchinson, 1937), p. 347.

a worldview, focus on its view of death. I learned this when sitting by the bedside of an atheist friend in hospital. He was suffering from a terminal disease and thus forced to face his own mortality. Unlike most people, at least he was willing to talk about this. In our conversation, I told him death is not the end.

'Shouldn't the possibility of an afterlife lead to a consideration of whether God might exist?' I asked him.

He looked at me in pain, not because he was offended, but more out of pity. 'You're such a good guy, Andrew. How can you believe all that disproved stuff?'

He then explained to me how death is natural. We are made up of atoms, which are basically energy. The first law of thermodynamics means energy is neither created nor destroyed. What it can do is change form. He assured me upon his death this would happen to him. 'And, Andrew, my afterlife will exist in the memory of the living.' He then smiled at me and said, 'So, don't forget me.'

It was a tender and agonizing moment.

For years I argued in my apologetics training courses that everyone fears death. Here is our opening to bring in the key tenets of our Christian worldview. But I've stopped saying this because I have met too many committed naturalists who genuinely do not fear dying. This accounts for why secular death rites celebrate the life of the deceased, keeping silent about the meaning of death and an afterlife. Death is no more than the termination of our biology, so all you can do is reflect on the short years of the deceased. Sadly, even Christian funerals can focus too much on being a 'celebration of life' rather than viewing death as the last enemy and therefore something to be properly mourned. But within this supernaturalist viewpoint we can also engage with a hope extending into the afterlife. Without such a perspective, death is disenchanted and either ignored or trivialized. This is an inevitable outcome of this form of worldliness.

Naturalism as the counterpart to theism

No believer can doubt that Christianity and naturalism are contra-
dictory. To be a Christian is to affirm a supernaturalist account of
reality. Sean M. Carroll – an advocate of naturalism – rightly sees
that:

> Naturalism is a counterpart to theism. Theism says there's
> the physical world and God. Naturalism says there's only the
> natural world. There are no spirits, no deities, or anything
> else.[15]

Here we see the active suppression of what naturalism doesn't want
to allow for. The sentence, 'There are no spirits, no deities, or anything else,' creates an exclusion zone for the bulk of what is relevant
for us as Christians. An exclusion zone is a territory where a sanc-
tioning body prohibits activities in a specific geographic area.
Naturalism does that to our faith, ripping the heart out of everything
we stand on.

'There are no spirits' includes angels and demons. It makes the
devil a figment of the imagination. Going further, it removes even
the reality of evil. Naturalism cannot substantiate this as a malevolent
force and makes it the mere outworking of organic processes.

With humans, the exclusion zone includes not having a soul.
There is no internal dimension to us that belongs to the spiritual
realm. That's why atheists such as Sam Harris deny that we have
free will and moral responsibility, making our actions determined
naturalistically.

That puts Christianity in total conflict with this entrenched dogma.
It creates a battleground because naturalism is an idea opposed to the
knowledge of God. One advantage is that naturalism is so at odds

---

15 'Maybe You're Not an Atheist – Maybe You're a Naturalist Like Sean Carroll', interview
in *Wired* by Eric Niiler with Sean M. Carroll, 9 May 2016, <www.wired.com/2016/05/
maybe-youre-not-atheist-maybe-youre-naturalist-like-sean-carroll>.

with Christianity that the incompatibility is clear. This makes it different from egoism with its kernel of truth. The self matters. But naturalism is the great lie! And despite its appearance of plausibility, there are contradictions. With some clear and capable thinking, it can be demolished – and many Christian thinkers have done this.

Testing the church for a diagnosis

Despite being the counterpart to the faith, I believe naturalism has contaminated the church. We may not have accepted its central thesis, but it has had an impact on how we view the world. Where egoism disorders our trust, naturalism disorders our vision. It ties us to the earth with a life based only on what we can see. Here is where our forgetfulness comes in. Christians today are losing a sense of spiritual reality because naturalism taints our vision. We cannot see the fullness of what we have in Christ. In his book *A Rumor of Angels*, the sociologist Peter Berger shows how the supernaturalist finds faith buffeted by the pressure of naturalism.[16]

So, how has the church let naturalism be smuggled in? I would suggest it happened without our noticing. Ours is a more soft denial of the supernatural – one that makes us functional naturalists. Of course, true 'believers' would never make a hard rebuttal, as that would turn us into unbelievers! Orthodox Christians continue to affirm supernatural truths – God's existence, the incarnation of the Son of God, Christ's physical resurrection from the dead. You can't get more anti-naturalist than that.

Our soft denials occur more on the level of insight. With supernatural realities no longer shaping our vision, the experience becomes distant. No longer can we enter into the fullness of our life in Christ. Under the influence of naturalism, our seeing is out of focus. That is why many Christians live with a kind of schizophrenia, where our

---

16 Peter L. Berger, *A Rumor of Angels: Modern Society and the Rediscovery of the Supernatural* (New York: A Doomsday Anchor Book, 1970).

minds are divided between the articles of our faith on the one hand and deeply naturalistic assumptions on the other. While the Bible may convince us in theory about the supernaturalist elements of our faith, the practical reality of them in our lives has become obscured. That's what I mean by a disordered vision.

What this means is that only what we see in first-order experience matters. We have lost sensibility for realities that stretch beyond ordinary perception. To say our insight is disordered is to say that something is wrong with the eye of faith. The seen has expanded, filling the horizon of our vision. The supernatural has become implausible for us too. We have become dull to eternal realities. These have become blurry, and we have forgotten how to live in them. The eyes of our hearts are not focused, and we have little sense for realities hidden from physical sight. In the words of Psalm 103, we 'forget . . . his benefits' (v. 2) because they're no longer real. This accounts for the symptoms we looked at earlier in this chapter.

Don't forget that how we perceive is more influential than how we conceive. We can have our theology in perfect order but live in a different perception of how things are. Blaise Pascal captured this idea when he said, 'The heart has its own reason that the mind knows nothing of.'[17] When something is wrong with our vision, we don't see what we should, and this can conflict with what our mind asserts as true. Today, we are failing to perceive and live in the spiritual realities central to our life in Christ, removing us from the realities he calls us to live in.

Our failure to live out our supernatural beliefs has devastating consequences for the church. For people like Ethan, it leads to the questioning of everything related to the faith. Other believers live with the loss by taking refuge in their theories and systems, ploughing on as if that is enough. For the majority, that will not be enough to hold them. With a paucity of spiritual reality, they are

---

17 Blaise Pascal, *Pensées and Other Writings* (Oxford: Oxford University Press, 1999), p. 157.

prone to the faintheart syndrome. Living with disordered vision means there is too little to sustain spiritual life. Not being grounded in realities that reach into the unseen makes them especially vulnerable when hard times come knocking. A failure of vision including the supernatural makes it hard to see how suffering fits inside God's providence and that one day he will make all things right. Without second-order vision it is hard to suffer well, and for many that will be the occasion for drifting away.

The treatment – seeing Jesus as Creator

What can cure our disordered vision and deliver us from this form of worldliness? We first need to recover a vision of Christ's transcendent majesty. Here is the secret to breaking through the ceiling of a naturalistic outlook – look outside creation, to the Creator!

To see Jesus is to be confronted with one whose being is beyond nature. Between Christ and the natural world there is an absolute boundary of being, the radical difference between the Creator and his creation. He is Uncreated Being – something science can't get its head around – and by way of contrast we are created beings. And as the One who transcends nature, Christ is the Divine Being who is incomprehensible. To believe this is to acknowledge that there are unlimited and hidden depths to him. Unlike scientism, which believes all the mysteries of nature will eventually be uncovered, here is one we will never fully grasp or uncover.

The incomprehensible God is a key aspect of his self-revelation in Scripture. Yes, he discloses himself, so we can know him truly, though always partially. But even in revealing himself, he remains the incomprehensible one because he transcends all that makes up this world – including nature. Nothing can measure him; nothing can contain him.

There are hidden depths to the Divine Being we will never know and understand – not even when we get to heaven. Here is someone so 'other' that our highest thoughts of him don't come close to under-standing him. He is not like anything we are familiar with. No wonder the Bible labours the point that there is no representation for the Divine Being. No image from our world can suffice.

The Jesus who dwells in his church temple is this God – the same person who asks Job:

> Can you fathom the mysteries of God?
>   Can you probe the limits of the Almighty?
> They are higher than the heavens above – what can you do?
>   They are deeper than the depths below – what can you
>   know?
> (Job 11:7–8)

Because of this, Christ forever remains the transcendent one, and to see him like this leads to genuine wonder. And when we live in wonder at who Jesus is, we can only worship with a response that asserts 'holy and awesome is his name' (Ps. 111:9). Naturalists often work hard to turn nature into something worthy of adoration, to turn our wonder at creation into worship of creation. But that wonder should direct us back to the Creator. Our worship of the Creator comes spontaneously, because of his real transcendent majesty.

Breaking up with naturalism

When the church sees Christ for who he is, it moves us beyond our natural ways of knowing. We perceive him like this only with the 'eyes of [our] heart' (Eph. 1:18). This alone will break the habits of naturalism. There is no way to domesticate the Son of God. To en-counter him frees us from formulaic reductions. It undoes us – just as it did the three disciples who got a glimpse of him on the Mount of Transfiguration (Matt. 17:1–8). The vision terrified them. They couldn't handle the experience – and yet they wanted more. 'Let's set up camp,' said Peter. We need the same undoing – to break us from the habit of reducing him to Christ Al-mate-y. Only then will we move beyond our pragmatism and our formulaic evangelical answers that think they make sense of everything.

When we have perceived Christ like this, it is hard to go back to the naturalist way of seeing. Once seared with his unsurpassable glory, we get a hunger and thirst for what this world cannot give. This is what we call the 'divine romance'. Our love isn't directed towards a theory but a person. As Chesterton is reported to have said, 'Let your religion be less of a theory and more of a love affair.'

Beholding Christ as he is makes our hearts burn with a fresh light so we perceive more than previously. As Jesus reminds us in John 17:3, 'Now this is eternal life: that they know you, the only true God, and Jesus Christ, whom you have sent.' It's an invitation to know the unknowable, and to respond is to worship with awe and wonder.

A vision of Christ's nearness

To be overwhelmed with wonder at the Christ who transcends nature never removes us from this world. And why? Because to see him for who he is includes the fact that he is Immanuel – God with us. As the incarnate one, here is the God who is immanent in the world, as well as transcendent. The apostle Paul holds the two together in 1 Timothy 3:16 when he breaks into a line of poetry and writes, 'Great . . . is the mystery of godliness: He was manifested in the flesh' (ESV UK).

That God became atoms and cells ultimately sets nature apart as full of wonder. When he became part of nature in the womb of Mary, Christ sanctified it in the most remarkable manner. Humans don't have to give special esteem to nature because Christ has already done it. Creation displays his glory in a real way because he is near. Gerard Manley Hopkins reminds us that 'Christ plays in ten thousand places'.[18] As the en-natured One, he is our licence to play in the natural

---

18 Gerard Manley Hopkins (1844–1889), from the poem 'As Kingfishers Catch Fire' (public domain).

world. Although Christians oppose naturalism, we are not pitted against nature, because Christ as Immanuel has made it all holy through his incarnation. We reject the idea in a well-known hymn that asserts that if we turn our eyes on Jesus, 'the things of earth will grow strangely dim'.[19] No – to know him is to delight in all he has made. We can truly enjoy creation for what it is, without spoiling created things by looking to them to give us ultimate meaning.

His being near is the guarantee that the natural and the supernatural are not separated but harmonized in a dance. At the same time, Christ both grounds nature and elevates it. Naturalism does neither.

To escape the worldliness of naturalism, we must recover the supernatural. Only then will we see with 'the eyes of [our] heart'. This requires an enlightening – just as Paul prayed in Ephesians 1:18 – one that will blow us away with a new vision of how things are. Only in beholding God will we cure our disordered vision and see him for who he is, restoring us to awe and wonder. Then spiritual reality will become ours – along with the hope and assurance that go with it. That allows us to trace his hand of Providence in the real world. But this higher insight into how things are will also be the end to our pragmatism. If the church is to find its way out of a disordered vision, we must passionately pray 'Be Thou My Vision, O Lord of My Heart'.[20]

Chapter summary

*Naturalism is a culture value operating in a closed universe perspective. This means there is nothing beyond the material, what we can see and touch. Science dominates this world, uncovering all its secrets. The contemporary church has accommodated this with a **disordered insight** that domesticates God and the faith that makes unseen and spiritual realities unreal. The consequence of this is a spiritual*

---

19 Helen Howarth Lemmel (1863–1961), 'Turn Your Eyes Upon Jesus' (public domain).
20 Mary Elizabeth Byrne (trans.) (1880–1931), 'Be Thou My Vision' (public domain).

weakness. To overcome this aspect of our worldliness, we must recover the sight of Christ who is both transcendent and immanent. Only this grants the wisdom to see deeper into reality.

Questions

- Is spiritual reality a problem for you? How, and what is the impact of this?
- When was the last time you thought about eternity and Christ's return?
- What is typical of the sermon applications you hear? If you preach or teach in church, how might you go beyond the 'five mores' in giving people a vision of Christ?

Further reading

C. S. Lewis, *Miracles* (Macmillan, 1953).

Francis Schaeffer, *True Spirituality* (Wheaton, Ill.: Tyndale House, 2001).

Michael Buckley, *At the Origins of Modern Atheism* (New Haven, London: Yale University Press, 2009).

Craig Gay, *The Way of the (Modern) World: Or, Why It's Tempting to Live as if God Doesn't Exist* (Grand Rapids: Wm B. Eerdmans, 1998).

Peter L. Berger, *A Rumor of Angels: Modern Society and the Rediscovery of the Supernatural* (A Doomsday Anchor Book, 1970).

5

Hedonism:
happiness is our greatest good

> If I find myself with a desire that nothing in the world
> can satisfy, the most probable explanation is
> that I was made for another world.
> (C. S. Lewis)[1]

Every human lives to be happy. That's why our desires are set on what we treasure. Our internal longing aims at something or someone that we believe will satisfy. Paul makes this point in Romans 8:5 when he says, 'the mind is set on *what* it desires' (italics added). The 'what' reveals our primary goals in life, and this works in the pursuit of our happiness project. If you want to understand yourself and others, there's no better place to begin than the quality and aim of our desires. We are very much what we desire.

The same is true of the church. Our health comes down to the depth of our affections and what we set them on.

Few Christians would disagree that Christ is meant to be our highest treasure and the source of our greatest happiness. But is he? Is our desire set on him above everything else? Look closely, and I think you will observe that all is not right at the level of our affections. Our love has become muddled. When the desires of the church become earthbound, she becomes worldly. A good indicator of this is when being entertaining becomes more important than something being meaningful.

---

1   C. S. Lewis, *Mere Christianity* (New York: HarperOne, 2001), p. 136.

Symptoms of a disorder

In your experience, would you describe church as 'deep'? Or has your experience of church been one of shallowness and emotional manipulation?

Because we are invited into relationship with Jesus, the church has received a meaning rich and full beyond measure. As Paul reminds us in Colossians 1:17, 'in him all things hold together'. That makes for a depth to the Christian life that is inexhaustible. With that being the case, the church should stand out as a space for profundity and richness. With Christ at the centre, believers should be stirred in their affections at the deepest level.

'Deep', however, is not something that marks the average church today. It's common for church to be dumbed down to 'Christianity Lite'. To be relevant, we even pride ourselves on keeping it practical and simple. Churches grounded in a more content-full tradition also tend to offer 'easy answers' rather than a word of genuine wonder as an invitation into the infinite delights of God and his creation. For many congregations, the norm on Sunday is a thought-for-the-day homily, no longer than twenty minutes, much like the pep talk you might hear from a life coach. It isn't uncommon to sense a repudiation of anything that sounds intellectual.

Even the church is often marked by biblical and theological illiteracy. Ask a believer today what 'justification by faith' is and they might look at you as if you're talking a foreign language. Why? Because theology has become a language the church doesn't understand. This is a recent shift that didn't characterize the generation of Christians my parents belonged to. Christians today struggle to read the New Testament letters without bewilderment. Beyond the Bible stories Christian parents read to their children, the church's engagement with Scripture is thin.

Shallow church

This shallowness in the church is why some are giving it up. Our attempt to keep it simple and practical has produced the conditions for starvation. Many are fleeing the shallowness because they hunger for more depth and reality.

Years ago, I was part of a convention for hundreds of church leaders. It was one of those glittery venues that made me think we were trying to replicate the Oscars. To wrap up the event, we all joined arms to celebrate our Christian unity. It was a rendition of the 'Hokey Cokey'. For those who don't know, this is a famous dance song that was a hit back in the day. Doing the 'Hokey Cokey' when you're squashed into a row of seats with fifteen inches of legroom is no easy feat – made harder when joined up with lots of other people. If I had an invisibility blanket, I would have used it to hide from shame and embarrassment!

Such a dumbing down is not because our intellectual capacities have suddenly become deficient. Rather, it mirrors what's going on in our culture. If I were to construct an epitaph for modernity, it might read like this: 'a culture of banality'. For reasons we shall explore in a moment, we live in a culture that is in a serious meaning crisis. Viktor Frankl was someone who saw modern people as living in an existential vacuum, what he called the 'abyss experience'.[2] We are languishing in a social milieu with insufficient depth to support our desires and hungers.

Sentimentality rules

To understand our banality and shallowness, we need to grapple with sentimentality – another symptom of something wrong in the church. And what do I mean by that? Sentimentality is a surface feeling lacking real substance. It's what we experience when watching

---

2   Viktor Frankl develops this thesis in his book *The Feeling of Meaninglessness: A Challenge to Psychotherapy and Philosophy* (Milwaukee: Marquette University Press, 2010).

an average film. We may be entertained by all the action and special effects, but beneath the surface thrill this generates there isn't much meaning. It lacks the depth and weight that art is meant for.

Being intensely moved is the goal, but that internal movement in our feelings is more for our benefit than a genuine response to something beyond us. Sentimentality is about generating an emotional experience that we can then consume. Note the emphasis on generating. For a culture committed to feeling good, this has become a perfected art. Philip Rieff described a modern person as one who is 'born to be pleased',[3] and that's what sentimentality caters to. It replaces profundity with intensity and always defaults to banality.

Showbiz Christianity

Our affections are genuine as they correspond to real events. Say your closest friend has struggled for years to get pregnant. When the tester kit generates a positive, your emotional response to that revelation is elation.

It is possible, however, for our feelings to be manufactured and conditioned. This often happens when people are being entertained in a crowd setting. The comedy skit or TED Talk may move you deeply, but often this movement in our feeling doesn't have much substance behind it. Such movement is in fact only superficial. This has become a feature of our gatherings. Doing church is about a show to be populated. The show is carefully choreographed to generate excitement. It's analogous to the film *The Greatest Showman*, chronicling the life of P. T. Barnum. The film ends with the words, 'The noblest art is that of making others happy.' To follow suit is to say, 'Let me entertain you.'[4]

Church has become part of the showbiz industry. This new kind of 'cool Christianity' begs the question, what it is really for? If it is to keep us entertained, then we have lost the plot. It is delusional to

---

3 Philip Rieff, *The Triumph of the Therapeutic* (Chicago: University of Chicago Press, 1987), p. 25.
4 *The Greatest Showman*, directed by Michael Gracey, December 2017.

think emotional intensity equates with profundity. Our services may move us, but if this is on the level of sentimentality, the outcome will not move us beyond the banal.

The holographic Jesus

When our gatherings are centred on sentimentality, Jesus himself becomes a hologram. These three-dimensional images are hollow – much like Abba's 'hologram concert', where they appeared as digital avatars rather than turning up in person. There is nothing substantial to these sentimental gatherings. While our corporate shows may bill him as the star attraction – someone to excite and thrill us – we do not make it clear why. He is merely part of the concert designed to stir us. The show is the key thing. Too easily we mistake the sentimental feeling for Christ himself. We could, however, exchange him for Elvis Presley or Ed Sheeran and it wouldn't make a difference to the event.

Jesus in the beauty and wonder of his character and work is not the reality that moves us, and there isn't enough in the hologram to secure our desire to him. Because the goal is entertainment, we end up losing our affection for Jesus. Intense feelings can only be stirred when the show is on, thus betraying a dysfunction in our desires. We become so accustomed to sentimental experience that our affections struggle to know what authentic longing is. When stuck in this loop, the default is to keep the theatrical going. We become addicted to the need for 'the show'. This generates the illusion that something profound is happening. That is why every gap in a service is filled with music – even during prayers.

I once spoke in a large church with Psalm 46:10 as my set text: 'Be still, and know that I am God.' After a twenty-minute eardrum-pounding performance, I got up to teach that quiet and stillness form the space where Christ is heard and known. The incongruity of the text with the 'show' was unplanned. It was an awkward moment for sure, and required a moment of humour to get over the hump.

Don't misunderstand me. I love a good show. But when church becomes a show, it muddles our affections.

Living in a virtue deficit

Another symptom of our disordered affections is a deficit in the church of 'virtue' – that is, of goodness, character and integrity.

We are what we desire, and we become like what we worship. We take on the image of what our longing reaches for. That means we become good in proportion to the quality, depth and aim of our desire. That is how critical our affections are!

For Christians, setting our affections on Christ is the key to becoming like him. Only then can his perfect virtue leave its mark on us. Conversely, when our desires become shallow and focused elsewhere, this will affect virtue negatively.

The same applies to the church gathered. We are what we worship corporately. One of the reasons we require the church to be a body is that our affections, habits and commitments are shaped in this community. Church cultures are orientated towards certain values too, so what's true of us individually is true corporately. That's why we can affirm that 'the church is what it loves'. And if what it really worships is numbers or relevance or money, it will become like a business or like entertainment, rather than like Christ. If our churches are shallow and sentimental, the whole body becomes removed from the conditions for becoming virtuous.

Sadly, the evidence for our loss of good character has become all too public in recent cases. Well-known leaders of churches and Christian organizations have been exposed for their lack of virtue. As Marcus Honeysett says in *Powerful Leaders*, 'We confuse confidence with competence, all the while neglecting character.'[5] Whether through sexual misconduct or serious abuses of power, we are

---

5 Marcus Honeysett, *Powerful Leaders? When Church Leadership Goes Wrong and How to Prevent It* (London: IVP, 2022), p. 14.

witnessing the toppling of our celebrities at a dizzying pace. All is not well on the virtue front.

The same decline is occurring in less public ways. No longer is the church a space where virtue flourishes and grows. The fruit of the Spirit is not being produced as it should be. In Paul's mind, the distinction between the non-virtuous and the virtuous was obvious, and clearly the church was to be producing the latter:

> The acts of the flesh are obvious: sexual immorality, impurity and debauchery; idolatry and witchcraft; hatred, discord, jealousy, fits of rage, selfish ambition, dissensions, factions and envy; drunkenness, orgies, and the like. I warn you, as I did before, that those who live like this will not inherit the kingdom of God.
>
> But the fruit of the Spirit is love, joy, peace, forbearance, kindness, goodness, faithfulness, gentleness and self-control. Against such things there is no law. Those who belong to Christ Jesus have crucified the flesh with its passions and desires. Since we live by the Spirit, let us keep in step with the Spirit. Let us not become conceited, provoking and envying each other.
>
> (Gal. 5:19–26)

Notice how Paul connects vice with the passions and desires of the flesh. If the church today is functioning in a virtue deficit, then that shows something wrong with our affections.

The diagnosis

The super-value making sense of these symptoms is hedonism. What is it, and how does it work?

For some it will conjure the image of a city trader snorting cocaine through a £50 note who then gets into a Ferrari with a gorgeous woman to drive to a three-star Michelin restaurant. Such a lifestyle is one that few can afford to indulge. But almost everyone today subscribes to this ideal – even if in less extravagant forms.

Hedonism is a way of life that places the highest value on sensory gratification – the kind our bodily senses deliver. By its light we live to be pleased – and the pleasure we're looking for is tied directly to our biology.

Hedonism is everywhere today. We see it in our sexualized culture where sex is promoted as the gateway to pleasure. It has countless other expressions too. From the high-end gastronomic meal to the hot tub, pleasure rules. From the excitement that shoots through the abdomen as our football team takes to the field, to the thrill of anticipating delivery of a new online purchase, pleasure is the goal. Whatever experience delivers a sensual thrill orients and shapes what our desire aims for. Hedonism is the pursuit of whatever dispenses it, defining what life is for.

To understand, we must examine how desire works. Humans exist in a complex mix of various desires that are 'wired in'. Each is first experienced as a deprivation. We desire what we do not possess, and it's the absence of something that makes us reach out for it. A single person looks for romantic intimacy on a dating site because of a privation of this in his or her life.

The three grades of desire

At the risk of an oversimplification, human desire can be graded into three kinds, each with an appropriate place in God's design.

The first and most basic class of human desire encapsulates the sensory ones. These desires are tied to our bodies operating on the level of the organic, and we share them with the animals. When Christians speak about these, they sometimes call them 'passions'. I prefer the word 'appetites' – a word we use in relation to food. Being hungry is a natural desire for a sustenance that will satisfy a bodily need.

One of my children illustrated this every day when he came home from school. I'd ask my son how school had been, and the comeback was, 'I'm starving.' That told me nothing about what had happened in class or on the school grounds. What it communicated was the all-consuming need of the moment. His appetites were driving everything, and a nutrient deficiency led him to believe that death was imminent! Organic desire prompted his emergency response – 'I'm starving.'

It made no difference that I knew he wasn't at death's door. I knew it was pointless to argue with this, so I'd make him a sandwich. What always amazed me was how in five minutes this child could move from a belief that he was dying of hunger to forgetting about it. Sandwich down the hatch, he skipped out of the door without a care in the world. It doesn't take much to satisfy our appetites.

Another example of a sensory desire is the experience of coming home from work after a ten-hour day. Your body experiences deprivation as exhaustion. With an overworked brain and a serious sleep deficit from the night before, your body is in protest mode, crying out for a break. So, slumping into your favourite chair, you vegetate for a while in front of the television, drifting in and out of consciousness.

We have different body-shaped appetites, and for teenagers and adults the sexual one is strong – and formidable. As desire pent up in the body, it makes its incessant demand for release.

The thing about our bodily appetites is that they have an automatic function. Being wired into our biology, they are not something we can choose to turn on or off.

It is important to stress that there is nothing inherently wrong with this kind of desire. If we didn't have them, we would die. The desire for food ensures we eat, the desire for rest ensures we sleep and the desire for sex keeps the world populated. Neither should we downplay the pleasure attached to our appetites. Christians some-times portray sensual gratification as the devil's invention. This is a mistake: God alone can take credit for these pleasures as part of his creation design. He intends us to enjoy such pleasures with thankfulness to him.

There are, however, reasons why we should view them as dangerous and keep them under control. If left untamed, they can ruin our lives. Our appetites must be domesticated by reason and virtue, and not allowed to rule over us.

The second class of desire is less connected to our biology and occurs in our internal life. These desires stretch us to goals that are more immaterial but no less essential for what it means to be human. Take the human longing to figure out how something works. Recently, when my cordless drill stopped working, I took it to pieces. Why? I wanted to discover the secret of a drill. Doing this offered no biological benefit, but it placated a curiosity – call it an intellectual satisfaction! For several years now I have desired to understand the mysteries of the money markets. This has little direct impact on my existence because I am not a trader, nor do I have considerable assets tied up in stocks.

Humans have inbuilt desires for the aesthetic – for story, visual arts and musical sound. Such pursuits aim at higher meaning. Without this class of desire – for truth and for beauty – human life would be impoverished. This is the human desire that makes a person yearn to play the violin or piano. Excelling at that, the individual may go further and practise for seven hours a day to become a professional. Such exertions don't meet a bodily need because something drives them on another plane. Here a deeper satisfaction can be experienced – as something that makes deeper sense of the world we live in.

The third type of desire is of the heart. This one goes to our very core and is meant for God alone. We have an inbuilt longing that nothing in creation can satisfy. This is our Creator's way of calling us to himself. He is infinitely happy and wants us to share this through a relationship with him.

Come, all you who are thirsty,
  come to the waters;
and you who have no money,
  come, buy and eat!
Come, buy wine and milk
  without money and without cost.
Why spend money on what is not bread,
  and your labour on what does not satisfy?
Listen, listen to me, and eat what is good,
  and you will delight in the richest of fare.
Give ear and come to me;
  listen, that you may live.
(Isa. 55:1–3)

When our core desire reaches out to the Lord, we attain the highest joy a human can experience. He satisfies a hunger for meaning that nothing in creation is capable of addressing. Because this desire is the deepest, it is the one that shapes us most decisively. As believers, we know our natural state is one of aversion to the God who invites us to share his happiness. This makes us fugitives in the world – and because it can't be satisfied here, we are deeply unsettled. As Augustine famously put it, 'Thou hast made us for Thyself and our hearts are restless till they rest in Thee.'[6]

Living under the shadow of the fall means all our desires have become disordered. There is a virus in our programming that has bent each kind out of shape. None of them works according to its proper order and each is disproportionate to what God intended. Hedonism is one way this occurs, by concentrating human longing on the first of our three levels of desire. Our life becomes ruled by the law of our appetites. These passions are in charge, and we must

---

6 Augustine, *The Confessions* (Indianapolis: Hackett Publishing Company, 1993), p. 3.

serve at their pleasure. As we shall see, this leads to a serious dis-ordering of what God intended our lives to be.

Hedonism is accepted as the goal for our lives and is positively endorsed in our culture as the way of life for everyone to pursue. Appealing to our affections, it calls us to be led by our appetites. In the words of the apostle John, it is living by 'the lust of the flesh' (1 John 2:16).

Hedonism on show

Hedonism is another 'in your face' ideal promoted everywhere and stimulated without shame or regret. The key impulse behind it saturates the imaginary of our culture. This comes with the message to live life to the full, and that means at the maximum of pleasure. It is a call to go with the desires of the flesh.

Futurama, the adult animated science fiction sitcom, gives us a funny example of this. Here, robots – selfless machines – are portrayed as hedonists. One robot, called Hedonismbot, is commonly seen sprawled out on a couch being fed grapes or having chocolate spilled over his golden body. There's also Bender, who loves hard drink, cigars and decadence. The humour comes from the irony of a non-organic entity such as a robot being portrayed as having organic appetites.

I hear hedonism beckoning in catchphrases like YOLO (you only live once) and *carpe diem* (Latin for 'seize the day'). Both are calls to live life to the maximum experience. By implication, it includes taking a risk if necessary. Let nothing hold you back. Life is short and you don't know what's coming tomorrow so suck the marrow out of it today.

Back in 2012, a rapper by the name of Ervin McKinness tweeted, 'Drunk af going 120 drifting corners – YOLO'. The 120 was miles per hour, and he died right after sending this tweet. But then, you only live once. If high-intensity experience in your body is the primary goal, then why wouldn't you risk your life to achieve it?

As we saw in chapter 2, the hedonism ideal is behind a lot of advertising campaigns. So many products use sex to promote them. A well-known, traditional, middle-of-the-road British retailer has done this with its indulgent 'food porn' ads. One features the image of a hot chocolate pudding being opened, leaving little to the imagination in terms of association. There are lots of appeals to sexual and food appetites, with an unambiguous invitation to indulge.

The sheer number of food programmes aired every night on television reveal what drives the affections of our Secular Age. Food critics fork delicacies into their mouths with palate descriptions that would do well in fantasy fiction novels. It is remarkable how much *carpe diem* can come from a mouthful of food. These broadcasts also highlight the place of the celebrity chef. They are in the highest echelons of our public heroes. You won't find an intellectual or a philosopher to rival them. Such public figures belong to a bygone age and are now replaced by the super cook.

A very brief history

It would be a mistake to see hedonism as a recent phenomenon. There has never been a moment in history when notorious individuals didn't make satisfying their appetites the goal of life. Take the celebrated nineteenth-century bad-boy poet Lord Byron. His hedonist lifestyle matched his literary career. It would be hard to imagine many who embraced the pleasures of the body as this poet did. For the ancient Greeks there was a special god who represented such a lifestyle. Dionysus was the god of wine and pleasure.

Where individuals have always felt the temptation to indulge the passions, there have been moments when whole civilizations have taken it on as a cultural value. That is why it is not unique to the Secular Age. The Russian sociologist Pitirim Sorokin saw what he called 'the sensate era'[7] in every civilization. The sensate is what occurs from the senses, the place from which the appetites operate. As he looked back on historical records, he observed that every civilization was hedonist in its final phase.

We often cite ancient Rome as an example from the past where historical records reveal the scale of its decadence as it embraced hedonism. In the century prior to the birth of Jesus there was a dramatic rise of this ideal for living. Bacchus was the god of wine, and a festival called Bacchanalia was a kind of state-sanctioned hedonism. It was an age that made gastronomy into a fine art, and the rich Romans revelled in their banquets. For the aristocracy, roast beef or barbecued lamb was too mundane, thus making way for novelty cuisine. It mirrors the spectacle in many of our contemporary cookery shows. Platters of peacock tongue and fried dormice chased down with litres of wine poured by naked servers. It is also striking that celebrity chefs became renowned and courted by the wealthy in that era. The parallels with our age are striking.

The steps to how our culture moved into this phase are complex and multifaceted. I believe we can trace some of its roots to the mid-nineteenth century. Freud, the Austrian psychologist, opened a door into the interior life of humans through psychoanalysis. Inside us is a mass of repressed memories, emotions and desires. These need to be released so we can grow up and come of age. Although Freud thought healthy people needed to delay gratification when it came to the pleasure principle of our bodies, he is partly responsible for what led to a full-blown hedonism. He opened the door to a greater awareness of what holds us back from being our true selves. His ideas also encouraged us to break free of authority structures that restricted our desires and longings.

Hedonism really came of age in the 1960s. A generation rose in reaction to what its parents stood for. This expressed itself in an

---

7   Ideas developed by Anne Glyn-Jones in *Holding up A Mirror: How Civilizations Decline* (Thorverton: Imprint Academic, 1996).

individualism that tried to break free of social conventions. It was time to let loose, grow your hair out and raise the hem of your skirt. And so the creed of sex, drugs and rock and roll was birthed – a statement of the revolution. Through the 1970s and 1980s, that same generation lost its mojo and committed to earning lots of money for a comfortable life. It may not have had the same edginess – no more lovemaking in public during rock festivals like Woodstock. But it was still hedonistic – made respectable and normalized. From then on it became entrenched in our culture as something to live for.

A taxonomy of hedonism

During the period in which the apostles wrote the New Testament, Rome was the dominant culture and solidly in its hedonist phase. That is why it is possible to detect hints of this form of 'the world' in the epistles. One of the clearest examples of this is in Ephesians 4:17–19, where Paul uncovers how it works with the precision of a neurosurgeon:

> So I tell you this, and insist on it in the Lord, that you must no longer live as the Gentiles do, in the futility of their thinking. They are darkened in their understanding and separated from the life of God because of the ignorance that is in them due to the hardening of their hearts. Having lost all sensitivity, they have given themselves over to sensuality so as to indulge in every kind of impurity, and they are full of greed.

This text uncovers two distinguishing characteristics of hedonism true for every age. Both focus on how it affects desire and affection.

The first thing we see is how this orientation reduces human life to the level of the sensate. It's what the little phrase 'given themselves over to sensuality' indicates. Here is a description of life lived on the level of the appetites. To exist like this means being like the animals and disregarding our unique human capacities: we lose 'sensitivity' to them.

Our family has a much-loved feline companion who lives this out to perfection. Biscotti (our three-legged cat) is a hedonist par excellence. When I stagger into the kitchen early in the morning, she harasses me for food. Having filled herself to the point of satisfaction, she then goes outside to play with her feline mates. After an hour of this indulgence, she demands to be let back in. Without so much as a thank you, Biscotti seeks one of her three favourite comfort spots for a long sleep. Her preferred choice in the winter is beside a radiator that also catches a bit of sun. In the evenings she has her cuddle lust where she wriggles over my book to get a prime spot on my lap. All she needs is tasty food, a warm and comfortable place to relax and a cuddle.

Paul reminds us here that when humans pursue the hedonistic ideal, it's the same impulse working itself out. As a super-value to orient our appetites, it becomes an irresistible seduction. We might describe it as a spell that puts us under its enchantment. When this kind of pleasure is trafficked as the only goal in life, it is hard to resist. Who doesn't want a good time? Our sensual desires are wired for this kind of experience. The underlying message of hedonism is, 'Don't resist your appetites; just give in to them.' That's what it means to be given 'over to sensuality'.

Over the years I've kept a note of how food establishments appeal to my sensual side in their advertising. Here are samples:

- Just say yes;
- Never say no;
- You just can't say no;
- Eat, Eat, and Repeat;
- The vehicle of happiness and bliss;
- This is your food heaven.

Part of the attraction of living for the sensual is that it's an effortless way of life. Unless you're naked in the middle of the Sahara, it doesn't take much exertion to hear the call of your appetites and answer it. If you're feeling hungry, just use the app on your smartphone and order to your door. Twenty minutes later it delivers its satisfaction. Apart from having to move from your living room to your front door, it costs you only the price on the menu. The same is true if you're feeling sexually aroused. Today you only need to make a few taps on your smartphone or laptop to find a site to satisfy your desire. The ease with which it finds contentment is also the danger point. Because so little stands in the way of gratifying our appetites, it's the easiest thing to give ourselves over to. Nothing higher or of significant weight can offer a resistance.

That is why convenience always takes over when we give in to this way of living. What we ignore is the destructive side to living by our appetites. If we give in to food, it can lead to obesity. If we give in to our sexual appetites, we can become porn addicts or worse. With nothing to withstand the orientation of the sensate, our appetites can get unruly and affect us negatively. As the character Pearl says in the Woody Allen film *Interiors*, 'You can live to be a hundred if you give up all the things that make you want to live to be a hundred.'[8]

Culture of banality

The second characteristic of hedonism that we see in Ephesians is that it leads to a life of banality. Paul is getting at this with the phrase 'having lost all sensitivity'. When our sensual side takes over, we live in the thinnest level of meaning. Our indulgences may deliver speedy pleasure, but this way of life leaves us restless and bored. Aldous Huxley spotted this and commented, 'Oh, how desperately bored – in spite of their grim determination to have a Good Time – the majority of pleasure-seekers really are!'[9]

---

8 *Interiors*, directed by Woody Allen, August 1978.
9 Aldous Huxley, *Complete Essays: Volume 2: 1926–1929* (Chicago: Ivan R. Dee, 2000), p. 363.

I once met a man who told me about his remarkable conversion to Christianity. Having been exposed to the Bible while growing up, he left it behind at university. His life was the success story most can only dream of. He climbed the ladder in an enormous media company, was earning a hefty income and embraced the ideal of the hedonist lifestyle. A fashionable social set, fast cars, lots of women and cocaine-laced parties – he was living the dream. Late one evening, drinking with a friend, he remarked, 'Isn't hedonism brilliant?!'

His friend's response was life-changing: 'This isn't hedonism, mate. It's nihilism.'

In that moment, the truth of that assessment struck him. Nihilism is a euphemism for life without meaning and a call to embrace chaos and disorder. So shocked was he by this assessment that he began a search that shortly after led to Christ.

Hedonism is a horrifying way of life because it closes down essential aspects of our internal life. It makes us numb to realities not directly tied to our biology. We become desensitized in a way that degrades us as humans. To paraphrase Paul's words, our thinking becomes futile, and we become darkened in our understanding and taken over by the ignorance within us. It may not be flattering, but it's true. When we operate on the level of the organic, we lose sensitivity to what extends beyond our appetites. Our minds corrode and we lose a capacity for great thought.

Hedonists reach a point where they can no longer be moved by the wonder of ideas. Reaching such a place isn't confined to those who live in opulent luxury. Netflix and ice cream or beer and video games can quite easily become ways of numbing ourselves to deeper meaning.

Here the banality factor comes in again. Someone I meet up with every few years is a hardcore hedonist. We go back a long way. He is enjoyable company with an 'off-the-scale' intelligence. Many years ago, this side of him was switched off as he pursued his life of pleasure. When we sit and have a beer, he warns me off if ever I go near the world of ideas. 'Don't make me think, Andrew.' He is now in a place where being thoughtful is being heavy.

This is not an atypical way to reason. As Ursula K. Le Guin writes, 'Which is better off, a lizard basking in the sun or a philosopher?'[10] The hedonist says it's definitely the lizard in the sun. Without clear thinking, we live in more and more irrationality. Os Guinness calls this the 'fit bodies, fat minds' syndrome.[11] What is true no longer matters, but only what delivers pleasure to the body. This amounts to living in a society described as 'post-truth'.

Unsatisfying

This leads to another characteristic of hedonism that Paul highlights: a life of constant consumption without the hope of a robust satisfaction. The end of verse 19 gets at this when it refers to people who have 'given themselves over to sensuality' and are 'full of greed'. This phrase could also be rendered as 'with a continual lust for more'. As our sensual appetites were never meant to satisfy us completely, and because we've given ourselves over only to them, we end up in a vicious cycle of consumption and craving. We devour what satiates our desire and, before we know it, the demand kicks in again. The longing that motivates the hedonist is unstable. As quickly as we get our fix, we need more.

Constantly consuming and never satisfied – that's how it works. We can see such an experience with those who are led by their sexual appetites. A release momentarily ends the sexual hunger, but quickly it kicks in again. The same happens for those who love to shop. It gratifies a desire, but after a few days the appetite for this form of consumption ramps up again. It sets up a cycle of 'shop till you drop' on constant repeat.

---

10 Ursula K. Le Guin, *Changing Planes* (Boston: Houghton Mifflin Harcourt, 2014), p. 162.
11 Os Guinness, *Fit Bodies, Fat Minds: Why Evangelicals Don't Think and What to Do about It* (Grand Rapids: Baker, 1994).

This kind of demand for a repeat of the experience poses the danger of escalation. Every time our appetite for shopping, sex or whatever reboots, we demand a little more in terms of what the experience delivers. It has to give something extra in terms of the pleasure 'oomph'. 'Greed' is a brilliant word to describe this. Never quite satisfied by the lusts of our flesh, we live as the unsatisfied at the deeper level of our humanity. The 'hunger and consume' way of living falls short and doesn't deliver enough to make us truly content. Constantly on the prowl for new amusements, we can never stand still to appreciate what we have. Hedonism proves to be an empty and exhausting way of life.

Testing the church for a diagnosis

As Christians, we may not be living the hardcore version of hedonism, but if we look carefully, we'll see a soft kind at work. A 'disordered affection' that has the hallmarks of hedonism afflicts us. Our desires are not functioning as God wants them to. We numb ourselves with sensual pleasures and forget our joy in Christ!

Becoming a Christian is all about a new kind of affection working in us – one directed to Christ. The eighteenth-century American pastor and theologian Jonathan Edwards wrote about this in his book *A Treatise Concerning Religious Affections*.[12] To be alive to Christ means being affected by him – an activation in the core desire of our heart. Because of who Christ is, it moves us in our affections at the deepest level. Being a follower of Jesus is being remade in how our desires work. The Holy Spirit intends our affections to be most intensely focused on Christ, so he is first in our heart and the one we love most.

Our hearts and their desires have become flabby and out of shape. Overgrown with weeds, our vitality is at a low ebb, and we settle for

12 Jonathan Edwards, *A Treatise Concerning Religious Affections* (Sydney: Wentworth Press, 2016).

too little. What C. S. Lewis said of hedonists could as easily be addressed to Christians today:

> We are half-hearted creatures, fooling about with drink and sex and ambition when infinite joy is offered us, like an ignorant child who wants to go on making mud pies in a slum because he cannot imagine what is meant by the offer of a holiday at the sea. We are far too easily pleased.[13]
> (from his sermon entitled 'The Weight of Glory')

Our muddled desires have forgotten the One who can satisfy our deepest longings.

The treatment – recovering Christ as the supreme good

What can cure our disordered affection and deliver us from this form of worldliness? Thomas Chalmers, a nineteenth-century Scottish professor, was on point when he talked about 'the expulsive power of a new affection'.[14] And what is this? It's like a toddler who can't get enough of watching CoComelon or another beloved show and throws a tantrum every time you turn the television off. In order to create a distraction, you pull her onto your lap with a favourite book. Now engrossed in you and the book, your child forgets about the television in the delight of this new experience. At this point, the expulsive power of a new affection has occurred.

This happens to us as followers of Jesus when we see him for who is. Christ is nothing less than the supreme good. For hundreds of years, philosophers debated where to find the *summum bonum*

---

13 C. S. Lewis, *The Weight of Glory and Other Addresses* (New York: HarperOne, 2001), p. 26.
14 Thomas Chalmers, *The Expulsive Power of a New Affection* (Wheaton, Ill.: Crossway, 2020).

(Latin for the 'supreme good'). It was Augustine who identified this with God, emphasizing the need for our hearts to be directed to him. Because Christ is the supreme good, there is nothing higher to aim for.

The desire of the church needs to be reorientated to the One who is truly the supreme good. He is the supreme good because he is good – perfectly good. Moses learned this when he asked the Lord God to show himself for who he really was in Exodus 33. The Lord's response comes in verse 19:

> I will cause all my goodness to pass in front of you, and I will proclaim my name, the LORD, in your presence. I will have mercy on whom I will have mercy, and I will have compassion on whom I will have compassion.

To see the Lord was to see goodness, because this expresses everything about him. What made up his goodness he spelled out to Moses as mercy and compassion. We could add other moral traits that rest on his goodness – faithfulness, kindness and truthfulness. Divine goodness ultimately expresses itself as love.

So, goodness is God's genuine character. He is originally good of himself and that means he doesn't need to work at being good because he is good – and has been eternally. Jesus had this in mind when he said, 'No one is good – except God alone' (Mark 10:18). He possesses this wonderful quality without limits. The Lord's goodness never changes in intensity because it sums him up perfectly. Psalm 119:68 makes the point in a pithy way by asserting, 'You are good, and what you do is good.'

Every good we enjoy as his creatures comes from this fountain. His creation is crammed with goods because it reflects him. And his goodness is best displayed in Jesus himself. Here is a being who totally and perfectly exhibits divine goodness. To see him like this has an impact on our affections – to the point of reordering them. He becomes what we live to love. We enter the experience of Isaiah and 'with joy . . . draw water from the wells of salvation' (Isa. 12:3).

Nothing higher to aim for

As the supreme good, he imparts a joy like nothing else. On the matter of joy and desire, C. S. Lewis is the best of guides. He wrote, 'God cannot give us a happiness and peace apart from himself, because it is not there. There is no such thing.'[15] No wonder Christ is to be first in our affections. He possesses in himself a boundless and overflowing joy that he wants us to share. That is what eternal life is all about. As Psalm 16:11 expresses it:

> You make known to me the path of life;
>> you will fill me with joy in your presence,
>> with eternal pleasures at your right hand.

Eternal life is not just life going on for ever. No, it is something of substance that can be experienced here and now. As Augustine stressed, eternal life is the supreme good.[16] It is life with God, which is sharing in a life of pure, unbounded joy. And as Lewis reminds us, 'Joy is the serious business of heaven.'[17]

The Bible is clear that we don't have to wait for heaven to enjoy this. Because of the expulsive power of a new affection, we can partake of this now. Christ offers us his joy on a moment-by-moment basis with the open invitation to 'taste and see that the LORD is good' (Ps. 34:8). Through the work of the Holy Spirit, we have constant access to Christ the supreme good. Being oriented in our desire to him is what elevates and reorders our affections.

---

15 C. S. Lewis, *Mere Christianity* (New York: HarperOne, 2001), p. 50.
16 Augustine, *Augustine: Political Writings*, translated by Michael W. Tkacz and Douglas Kries (Indianapolis: Hackett Publishing Company, 1994), p. 146.
17 C. S. Lewis, *Letters to Malcolm: Chiefly on Prayer* (London: Geoffrey Bles, 1964), p. 122.

Here is what Paul is getting at in Galatians 5:16–17:

> So I say, walk by the Spirit, and you will not gratify the desires of the flesh. For the flesh desires what is contrary to the Spirit, and the Spirit what is contrary to the flesh. They are in conflict with each other, so that you are not to do whatever you want.

When we desire what the Spirit wants then we are directed to Christ as the supreme end for our affections. The Christian is someone who knows the truth of this – and has access to it.

When the church engages with Christ, not as a hologram but as the supreme good, it makes all the difference to us as desiring beings. Our corporate gathering week by week needs only to focus our affections here. He is enough to provide us with an emotional satisfaction that is meaningful and grounded in deepest reality. The reality for most Christians is that at best we get only intermittent experiences of this highest joy on offer. However, once our affections have tasted of Christ, we carry a wound in our hearts that never goes away.

We see a metaphor of this in the Old Testament book Song of Songs. The Beloved expresses desire as a kind of sickness – 'sick with love' (Song 2:5; 5:8 ESV UK). Here is a desire that keeps its vibrancy even when it is not quenched. Deprivation only makes one long the more, so the desire increases. What is for certain is that when our affections have tasted Christ the supreme good, there is no returning to the slums where our desires used to play. Tasting of the One who satisfies our deeper longings changes everything, and with this comes the burden of not being able to turn back.

Tasting the reality of Christ and his infinite joy changes our relationship to the world. With him at the centre, we can appreciate all the goods of creation. When we have Jesus as first in our heart, we find him reordering the other desires we carry. Our internal desires for knowledge, for good and for beauty, and our sensory desires (for food and for sex) begin to function as he intends them. And because our affections are working in a proper hierarchy, our 'meaning crisis' is resolved. Everything finds its proportionate meaning in relation to Christ as our ultimate meaning. In him we know that the gifts of creation are genuine goods for our enjoyment, but they are not ultimate goods. One who has tasted Christ the supreme good can never forget this order. As C. S. Lewis so eloquently stated:

> put first things first, and we get second things thrown in; Put second things first and we lose both the first and second things. We don't even get the sensual pleasure of food at its best when we are being greedy.[18]

Let me stress again that having our affections set on Christ does not remove us from the world. Some Christians have thought that desiring Christ above all somehow removes us from the here and now. Wearing hair shirts, eating inedible food and praying at all hours of the day and night is not how we are meant to live. When our love gets reordered so that Jesus is first in our affections, the surprise is that we find a new freedom to enjoy all the pleasures he sends us our way – including the sensual ones. Because he is first in our affections, we receive every good thing as his gift with a thank you. It reorders our affections into what God always intended – set on him.

Given that Christians are what they desire and love, we come back to where these find their focus and aim. Are the affections of our heart set on him above everything, or are we living in a disordered affection? To escape this form of worldliness today, the church doesn't need more light shows. The stronger spell to wake us from the enchantment of the world is Christ as our supreme good. That aim is anything but banal. Indeed, so weighty is he as the good that no words can suffice. The best of our worship and adoration falls short. We may

---

18 C. S. Lewis, *Collected Letters*, Volume 3, collected and arranged by Walter Hooper (New York: HarperCollins, 2009), p. 111.

even become silent. And the reason we gather as the church is to inflame and stir this desire.

Chapter summary

*Hedonism is a culture value that encourages us to live by our appetites alone with the promise that this is the way to achieving the pleasures God made us for. The contemporary church has accommodated this with a **disordered affection** that has displaced Christ for more immediate sources of satisfaction. Our corporate life has been reduced to entertainment, and we have become sentimental and banal, with a diminishment of our God-directed desires. To overcome this aspect of our worldliness, we must recover our knowledge of Christ as the supreme good, who alone is the source of our highest happiness, and who orientates us to ultimate meaning.*

Questions

- What do you really desire, if you're honest? What is most influential in shaping your desires?
- Has your church experience deepened your character and strengthened your virtue?
- If you were to stop attending church, would that significantly affect your desire for Jesus?

Further reading

James K. A. Smith, *You Are What You Love: The Spiritual Power of Habit* (Grand Rapids: Brazos Press, 2016).

Anne Glyn-Jones, *Holding up A Mirror: How Civilizations Decline* (Thorverton: Imprint Academic, 1996).

Augustine, *The Confessions* (Oxford: OUP Reprint Edition, 2008).

Victor E. Frankl, *Man's Search for Meaning: The Classic Tribute to Hope from the Holocaust* (London: Rider, 2004).

6

Politicism: everybody wants to rule the world

> The devil always sends errors into the world in pairs –
> pairs of opposites. And he always encourages us to spend
> a lot of time thinking which is the worse. You see why,
> of course? He relies on your extra dislike of the one error
> to draw you gradually into the opposite one.
> (C. S. Lewis)[1]

Are we the bad guys? It can often feel that way for Christians today. The tide has turned, making it uncomfortable to be known as followers of Christ. Not so long ago I experienced this in an interaction with someone in my home town of Cambridge. Having just heard a public talk by a famous academic, I got into a conversation with the person next to me. Half an hour later we were the only two in the lecture theatre. Our connection was profound, and we ranged back and forth over the content of the talk we'd just heard.

When I mentioned in passing that I was a Christian, his face blanched. For several seconds there was an awkward silence between us. He then found his voice and expressed genuine shock. 'You seem like a decent chap, Andrew. How can you possibly believe in something so nefarious, an ideology that has produced such injustice throughout history?'

That was the end of our conversation. Clearly, I was on the wrong side of the good, and in his mind everything I stood for was incompatible with the new moral order.

---

1   C. S. Lewis, *Mere Christianity* (New York: HarperOne, 2001), p. 186.

Unfortunately, Christianity's bad reputation isn't entirely without substance. Looking back, it's clear that the church hasn't consistently been shaped in a Christlike manner in the way it has engaged with social issues. That's why our collusion in slavery, racism, homophobia, misogyny and a disregard of the environment are such serious failings.

Given that these are matters that dominate today, it's hard not to feel the weight of the claim for justice in the new moral order. And it is the weight of this pressure that makes the church work hard to gain approval. As our reputation declines, we want to convince the world that Christians are on the side of the good. We might point to the work our church does in caring for the poor, supporting families, recycling and using fair trade goods, campaigning for social justice.

Of course, that's not wrong! Throughout history, being good has been an essential aspect of the church's witness to the watching world. The issue is more who sets the agenda for what it means to be good – Christ and his Word, or contemporary culture?

Today, the Secular Age has redefined how our culture sees the moral good. The society we live in believes it has 'progressed' to a better place than the traditional norms Christians live by. That is why, if we're faithful to the Bible, we find we're on the wrong side of lots of issues that matter. On subjects like sex, marriage, abortion and end-of-life issues, believers no longer occupy the moral high ground.

Only a few decades ago, those outside the faith viewed us differently. In a benign way, we were the goodies. 'Ah, bless them,' they'd say, 'they don't do sex before marriage.' Now the tables have turned. Being a Christian is no longer to be counted with being principled people. We have a reputation that makes us the immoral of our society – narrow-minded and bigoted, and with biblical teaching as harmful. Sadly, evangelicals have sometimes fed this narrative by reflecting an ugly orthodoxy that hasn't demonstrated the love of Christ, as we'll explore in more detail.

What has your experience been of how churches are dealing with this? How are we responding to the growing gap between the church and people's views today of goodness and justice? How are we responding to the growing opposition and pressure? And who is giving the lead on how we work for justice? Surveying what's going on today, I see unhealthy trends that are symptoms of another form of worldliness.

Symptoms of a disorder

An overly polarized Christianity

A striking symptom of something wrong is how polarized Christianity has become. Many identify faith unambiguously with a particular moral and political agenda.

This isn't so much about the party and voting but how the church engages with what has become known as the culture wars. James Davison Hunter is a Christian sociologist who coined the term 'culture wars'.[2] His point was to show how this battle functions as conflicting visions of how we are to live our life together. Going far beyond private opinion, here is an ideological warfare to define the heart of America. It is a struggle to dominate the cultural institutions of power that shape the centre. Recently, the culture wars have spread to Europe and the battle rages for the soul of the West.

The church, too, has signed up for military service. In different ways we are investing in the new political struggle to shape society – and this warfare is defining our core commitments. Such an outlook inevitably pushes the church to alliances that end up compromising us.

---

2 James Davison Hunter, a sociologist at the University of Virginia, introduced the expression in his 1991 publication, *Culture Wars: The Struggle to Define America* (New York: Basic Books, 1991).

Allegiance to either side of the culture wars becomes a test of faithfulness. We are forgetting that allegiance to Christ and the transformative power of his kingdom is how the world is substantively changed for good.

Echoing the culture

As the cultural pressure ramps up, many in the church have joined the contemporary crusade for justice in line with the new moral order. As our society jettisons the old Christian morality as not fit for purpose, many believers are shifting their position on matters like sex, marriage and gender. This includes taking up the causes for justice of our times – Black Lives Matter, same-sex marriage and transgender rights. Fighting for justice along these lines is viewed as faithfulness to Christ and consequently given great weight.

What makes this prone to accommodation – and therefore a form of worldliness – is that the terms of engagement are set more by culture than by Christ and Scripture. The current movement for justice exercised in parts of the church has parallels with the social gospel movement that was prominent in the USA from about 1870 to 1920. Social reform became the main thing, but it ended up squandering the fundamentals of the faith.[3]

Culture warring

Another response takes Christians down the opposite path. Aggrieved by all the cultural decay, they pit themselves against the 'heathen' of our age and move into fight mode. Marked by disgust, they come across as self-righteous, as if the degradation is a personal affront to their honour. Spend an hour with Christians in this camp and you're likely to hear a study in gloom.

While the accommodation option may pose the more obvious danger as it moves from the authority of Christ and his Word, no one

---

3   Argument developed in Joseph Bottum, *An Anxious Age: The Post-Protestant Ethic and the Spirit of America* (New York: Image, 2014).

should be blind to the danger of a hate-filled reaction. When the church pits itself against ruling establishments and those who back them, we remove ourselves from the possibility of being true salt and light.

Once we've made our diagnosis, we'll return to this 'great divide' and look to understand these subjects better in the light of the underlying issues of worldliness.

Avoiding the issues

Here is the response where Christians withdraw into their little ghetto. I call this the 'flight brigade'. The scale and pressure of the current moral shift is so bewildering that some have retreated into the bunker. Like the proverbial 'burying our heads in the sand', they avoid engaging with these huge cultural changes. Motivated by timidity, they view the current mess as too complicated and a quiet withdrawal as the best course of action.

I have talked to pastors who advocate such an approach, citing a desire not to put up unnecessary barriers to the gospel. What the flight brigade don't recognize is how the social imaginary works. Ignoring the clamour does not make cultural values go away. I suspect that in the bunker many Christians are inadvertently being compromised, giving way to the ideals that make up the new moral consensus. Such a response makes believers passive and unable to resist. That's why avoidance is also a form of worldliness. Both the fight brigade and the flight brigade are unhelpful responses – even if they do appear to be more faithful than accommodating.

The diagnosis

The super-value giving rise to these symptoms is what I am calling 'politicism'. Here is an ideal asserting that political factors dominate everything else as a medium for making the world right. What makes politicism so dangerous is its parody of how sin and redemption work. In his book *Political Visions and Illusions*, David T. Koyzis highlights how political idealism has a sin narrative that 'locates the source of evil not in our rebellion against God and his word, but in something structural in his creation'.[4] What's wrong with the world is in the social realm.

Such a rendering of the problem disregards the Bible's view that sin has warped humans from the inside out. Although sin does distort the social realm and structures, the ultimate root cause is personal and an act of our mutiny against God. Because politicism defines the problem as something structural in the social realm, so the solution must come from there. That is why every political ideology has its own salvation narrative. Koyzis writes about:

> ideologies (political) based on a specific soteriology, that is, on a worked-out theory promising deliverance to human beings from some fundamental evil that is viewed as the source of a broad range of human ills, including tyranny, oppression, anarchy, poverty and so forth.[5]

If politicism diagnoses the fundamental problem incorrectly, so too will its solution to bring redemption. Losing sight of the real problem means losing sight of the greater answer. A complete salvation won't come ultimately through pursuing justice – as politicism asserts. It is through Christ and the salvation he offers via the establishment of his kingdom and rule, a rule that includes the transformation of people and not systems.

A very brief history

Being politicized means we forget that Christ does not need the backing of the state to get the job done. He doesn't require Constantine for

---

4 David T. Koyzis, *Political Visions and Illusions: A Survey and Christian Critique of Contemporary Ideologies* (Illinois: IVP Academic, 2003), p. 29.
5 Koyzis, *Political Visions and Illusions*, p. 29.

his kingdom to flourish. Here I refer to the Edict of Milan in AD 313 under Constantine the Roman Emperor. In the long struggle between paganism and Christianity, this political edict was decisively in favour of the church. With the backing of the state, the church was able to march forward into an age of great cultural influence.

No doubt the church has used this power for both good and bad, but the Edict of Milan set up a dynamic where Christians easily default to co-opting the power of politics to push the cause of Christ. The political kingdom is confused with Christ's kingdom, thus politicizing the faith. But to be overly politicized is always a compromise because it confuses the city (*polis*) of humankind with the city (*polis*) of God. When the political becomes the focus for how we exert influence and power, it makes us earthbound so we lose the sense of our belonging to Christ and his kingdom. They are not the same, and the church that knows the difference will be best placed to change the world.

Politicism today has its roots in secular humanism, whose history we also touched on in chapter 3. This is based on a presupposition that only humans can determine a better moral order for society. Secular humanism operates from a commitment to progress – that the present must be better than the past. As our culture retreated from its Christian foundations, the establishment of a new moral order was inevitable. This would consolidate the Secular Age, leading it to the promised land. What is striking is how much was invested in the political spectrum to achieve this. Secular humanism was committed to reversing the fourth-century struggle between Christianity and pagan Rome. Where the Constantinian settlement made the public square one that gave political clout to the church, our age has endeavoured to make the public square secular and ruled by our better political judgments.

We see this during the Enlightenment, where a new kind of liberty was secured for individuals – one with the backing of the state.[6] Most

---

6   Argument developed by Patrick J. Deneen in *Why Liberalism Failed* (New Haven: Yale University Press, 2018).

of the liberty championed in the early phases of the humanist project worked in favour of white European males, and it took a long time before women and people of colour were the recipients of benefits. But as time passed, various political reforms extended this liberty, beginning with the abolitionist cause to end the slave trade that European empires had exploited for centuries. Women found new political freedoms in the early twentieth century with the Suffragist and Suffragette movements. This granted them the vote, and slowly the nations of the West adapted. The decriminalization of homosexuality also occurred in the twentieth century. One change at a time, new liberties were being granted to groups who had been oppressed.

The political freedoms and rights obtained in the Secular Age can be an uncomfortable truth for Christians to grapple with. Why didn't the church campaign for these matters when it had the political clout to bring social justice to those in chains and without a voice? Of course, many conveniently overlook that the abolitionist cause was led by Christians. In the early eighteenth century, a remarkable American by the name of Benjamin Lay engaged in raucous anti-slavery activities. Later in the same century, the English parliamentarian William Wilberforce did the same, leading to the Slave Trade Act in 1807.

For several centuries, Western society kept much of the scaffolding of the old moral order rooted in the Bible. Marriage and sexual ethics were left untouched. That has changed in the past few decades. Now the pace of moral reform has sped up, backed up by the power of the state in newly enacted laws. Legislation allowing for same-sex marriage is an obvious example. As the new moral order conflicts with much of what Christianity stands for, the church is now in the public eye and the pressure for us to accommodate ramps up.

The great divide

As the new moral order abandons its Christian roots, the West now finds itself involved in a great political divide. Here is where the culture wars are being fought. While the mainstream embraces the new moral order, there has been significant pushback. For a sizeable number, the progressives have gone too far, and now is the time to put up a resistance. It would be hard to overstate the gulf between the two sides in these culture wars. There isn't even a middle ground to occupy, leaving everyone with what appears to be a stark either/or choice. Across the divide is a lot of political grievance and name-calling. Whether via media outlets or in conversations with a neighbour, it is not uncommon to hear invectives like 'woke' or 'alt-right' thrown around.

In an attempt not to be pejorative, I'm calling the two sides the *radical progressives* and the *reactionary conservatives*. Both are committed to politicism and share the belief that the social spectrum is where the problem lies, and any solution must also focus there. It is how the problem and solution are defined where everything becomes so polarized. Understanding the great divide is important for the church because we have become separated along similar fault lines. And that is a sign of our present worldliness – more distinguished by our political outlook than by Christ and the distinctiveness he calls us to.

The radical progressives

Those aligning themselves with the radical progressives see history as the outworking of a conflict between the oppressor and the oppressed. Behind this lies an ideology known as 'critical theory'. All relationships are viewed through the lens of abusive power where the strong prey on the weak. The oppressed are those on the wrong side of gender (non-male), race (non-white), sexual preference (non-heterosexual) and disability (non-able-bodied). The American scholar John McWhorter describes the agenda of the radical progressive like this:

> Battling power relations and their discriminatory effects must be the central focus of all human endeavor, be it intellectual,

moral, civic, or artistic. Those who resist this focus, or even evidence insufficient adherence to it, must be sharply condemned, deprived of influence, and ostracized.[7]

Inflamed by a powerful sense of grievance, the radical progressives have a revolutionary mindset for justice. Their crusade has raised a vast army – sometimes disparagingly called SJWs (Social Justice Warriors) – with different organized divisions for getting justice for the oppressed. On the matter of racial discrimination there is the Black Lives Matter (BLM) movement. LGBTQ+ emphasizes sexual diversity and fights for the rights of this community.

Because humans are wired for justice, the radical progressives have great appeal. Everybody wants to play their revolutionary part in changing the world. Joining this moral crusade comes with the allure of overturning centuries of power abuse. It presents itself as open-minded and tolerant against a backdrop of bigotry and oppression. No wonder it has such an attractive face! If two people of the same sex are in a loving relationship, why would we deny them marriage? If someone feels that their true self is expressed by a gender identity that is different from their sex 'assigned at birth', why would we deny them both the social support and medical interventions to live according to that identity? If someone with a debilitating illness chooses a 'suicide tourism' trip to Switzerland, why should we stop them, given the suffering they bear? The progressives say we shouldn't judge people for their choices and should support and celebrate each person living out their own self-expressed identity.

Identity politics

What has invigorated the cause of the radical progressives is the degree to which they have politicized justice. That's why it fits politicism as an ideal. Human identity and personal choice have

---

7   John McWhorter, 'What Kind of People', in *Woke Racism: How a New Religion has Betrayed Black America* (Rugby: Swift Press, 2021).

become wedded to political rights and freedoms. The term to describe this is 'identity politics'. What fundamentally defines people's identity is the political justice matters they have given themselves to. If it's BLM, then race defines them; if it's the transgender cause, then being non-binary defines them. And because justice is so tied to identity, it makes real debate about the issues personal rather than moral.

Progressive morality on show

We don't have to look far to see the radical progressive agenda in play. Watching the news, a film or a television drama typically exposes us to its ideology. We are bombarded with a constant stream of scenarios raising awareness of all the issues, and this normalizes them.

An average sitcom could well have two people of the same sex living in a nice suburban house with a beautiful child. For the majority this raises no discomfort, but for most evangelicals it does. Straightaway we feel on the wrong side of the moral consensus. The issues are broadcast in such a way that we are the immoral ones. Such is true of so many issues belonging to the progressive cause. From how we view our colonial history to what we do with the environment, we are bombarded by a host of moral matters.

The reactionary conservatives

On the other side of the great divide are the reactionary conservatives. It is from this quarter that the pushback arises. Here is the group that looks with horror at a society that is rapidly changing.

Being conservative means that change is generally viewed with suspicion. Such an outlook tends to portray the past nostalgically. In the past our nation was a better place to live and raise our children. Donald Trump's famous MAGA (Make America Great Again) is straight from this playbook. The past represents a 'golden age' that was good because there was a different political mindset. The present is terrible because of what the liberal left have done to it.

Such an outlook roots the problem of sin in the transformations brought on by 'the left'. The way of salvation is to restore things to how they used to be. So stop the rot by opposing the progressives tooth and nail, and let's restore the past to what it was by taking back political power.

A taxonomy of politicism

If the church is to overcome politicism, we must understand how it works. Today it is marked by three characteristics.

The righteous intuition

First, it works from the moral high ground with an absolute certainty of being correct in the political cause it embraces. The cultural psychologist Jonathan Haidt has explored how this works in his book *The Righteous Mind: Why Good People are Divided by Politics and Religion*.[8] He attempts to give a reason why we are so socially and politically divided. Haidt asserts that our political and moral beliefs are fashioned more by intuition than by reason. Existing in the felt realm (rather than thought through), it comes from the gut and is visceral. That makes us emotive in how we engage with political matters today. The overused word 'woke' highlights this. The key to normalizing social and racial justice is inculcating a heightened awareness. Awareness is important, but if it's only intuition, then there's a danger. Right awareness depends on right-mindedness. By appealing to feeling and intuition, politicism engages with soft power with great success. Both the progressives and the conservatives know how to play on this.

Because politicism tends not to be reasonable, the causes espoused can be full of contradictions. Political instincts that work from the gut make followers highly gullible. We can see evidence of this in

8   Jonathan Haidt, *The Righteous Mind: Why Good People are Divided by Politics and Religion* (London: Penguin, 2013).

some of the conspiracy theories that abound on both sides. The QAnon phenomenon on the part of some reactionary conservatives is one of the more extraordinary illustrations of this.[9]

Being driven by intuition and feeling also makes politicism prone to anger at the other side. That's why disgust and outrage are dominant features of the culture wars today. All this negative feeling makes for a toxic environment. When the church gets caught up in this grievance, our witness is tarnished and we cease to be outposts of light, hope and joy that reflect Christ.

Because political allegiances are so visceral, it becomes impossible to get any perspective of the other side. The progressives and the conservatives embrace their cause as right and simply write off the other without any attempt to understand their viewpoint. While the radical progressives like to present themselves as the more tolerant way, a darker reality is at work. It's a political and moral viewpoint that offers tolerance only for those who agree with it. Failure to fully 'buy in' is met with fury. Here is where Christians face opposition and pressure to conform. We must accept their new moral order or face the music.

But the conservatives are no less hostile in their political reaction. Here is where many in the church today are stuck. For those who take their stand on the Bible's authority, the morally conservative standpoint is the more natural allegiance. But once this alliance is established, the visceral antagonism tends to take over. Reacting like that compromises Christ's invitation to be his loving and faithful presence in the world.

Crowd-based

Humans are groupish, with a strong desire to belong to the right crowd. In the current political climate, everyone must choose an allegiance to one side, which then opens up a chasm. To belong to

---

9   A large movement that believes in a conspiracy concerning a deep state of elite Satan worshippers in government, business and media.

the progressives or the conservatives becomes a zero-sum game. You must fully embrace the political cause as one of the faithful. And the visceral way in which the new politicism works adds to what Douglas Murray calls 'The Madness of Crowds'.[10] It makes for a lot of negative profiling of the other side – right-wing bigots, white supremacists, left-wing loonies, cultural Marxists. Our social media platforms are where we meet our crowd and the outlet for expressing our grievance. Because social media uses algorithms that herd us to sites where everyone thinks like us, the only people listening are the crowd we've aligned with. What we're left with is a lot of noise.

A lumping judgment

Another characteristic of how politicism works is that it bundles disparate moral issues into a oneness. I call it a 'lumping' judgment. Each side presents its cause as a package with the demand that we accept them all.

I know what it's like to be on the receiving end of this. Part of my work is to host lunches for academics where the table is open to conversations on a variety of subjects. There is no agenda except to take people's concerns and questions seriously and let the dialogue unfold. Many who take part are not Christians, and they are rich and fruitful occasions.

In one of these discussions, I made a passing reference to the Bible's view of marriage. This didn't go down well because it set off a minor tremor which, after a few minutes, increased to a seven on the Richter scale. By the end of the tirade they had charged me with being homophobic, a racist, a misogynist and a climate-warming denier. No doubt I have biases and prejudices, but this was jumping to a whole lot of uncharitable conclusions without knowing my actual views or relationships. My wife could write a book on my many

---

10 Douglas Murray, *The Madness of Crowds: Gender, Race and Identity* (London: Blooms-bury Continuum, 2019).

faults, but I don't think misogyny would be one of them. I am also active in creation-care matters. None of this mattered to those who heard my view of marriage and assumed the rest.

This same lumping tendency is how the reactionary conservatives work. To express a conviction that racism and misogyny are ongoing matters requiring justice is to set yourself up to be cast as a leftie, a cultural Marxist and someone who believes in gay marriage.

It's important to note that this 'lumping' tendency is an added complexity for Christians as we engage with culture. Each issue in the bundle is unique and requires thoughtful consideration. Climate change will take us down one line of enquiry while racism will necessitate another.

Testing the church for a diagnosis

Rather than letting Christ set the agenda for our priorities of social engagement, the political realm is doing that. And when the church uncritically aligns itself with a political agenda, it becomes worldly, whatever side we take. To do that is nothing less than a disordered allegiance, one that fails to honour Christ and his plan for our lives above all else. To see how this has occurred, we only need to observe how the church has been shaped by the contours of the culture wars. The evidence for this can be seen in the great divide now present among the followers of Christ. Whether on the right or the left of the culture wars, one's political outlook has come to define what it means to be the faithful.

Among many evangelicals in the USA, being faithful is seen as a commitment to the Republican cause. The only real danger is the radical left and critical theory. Donald Trump may get a light critique for not being such a wonderful moral example, but nothing is said about the grasp for power and the undermining of democratic processes. On the other side there are a growing number of Christians who look in horror at the right. They are aghast how any genuine follower of Christ could ever vote Republican. That makes being a Democrat the litmus test of the faithful.

In Europe, the divide among Christians isn't so much party political but in how we align ourselves with causes – climate change, Black Lives Matter and so on. Believers on the more progressive side see conservative Christians as locked in bigotry and ugly orthodoxy. It isn't uncommon for them to see everything they stand for as an embarrassment to the cause. Similarly, conservative Christians are appalled at the perceived moral compromise of the left.

Alongside the growing divide, politicism shows itself in the church along the lines of the taxonomy we looked at earlier. The moral and political judgments of Christians often operate viscerally rather than reasonably. One outcome is that outrage and disgust are now operating inside the church. And as political alliances harden, the levels of angry rhetoric increase. Among believers it is common to observe lumping judgments at work. Being mired in politicism, Christians also fail to perceive that politicism undermines the gospel. Too easily we buy into the problem of sin being fundamentally social, and tone down the good news of Christ's death and resurrection to overcome our rebellion against God.

For lots of reasons, politicism as a super-value is a sobering challenge for the church today. And it poses a real test of our allegiance. For Christians who tend to the progressive side, the challenge is staying faithful to the authority of Christ. Your leaning may take the appearance of a nicer-looking Christianity, but does Jesus fit into it as agreeably as you think? The danger of aligning on this side is compromise. Often the Bible is ignored or reinterpreted to allow for matters like same-sex relationships and gender reassignment. The authority of the new moral consensus eclipses the authority of Scripture to shape our minds on the issues confronting us. Those who uncritically side with the radical progressives are in danger of being swept away. Being so like the world, they could well become like the ten lost tribes of Israel and disappear from the church altogether.

But while there is reason to be cautious of what Christian progressives are committed to, the church should not be blind to their justice pursuits. Abuses of power, whether in the church or in society, must never be matters of indifference. Racism is a great evil, as are misogyny and discrimination against those with same-sex attraction. In Christ's name we are called to pursue justice. We stand within a worldview that provides the true basis for overcoming discrimination. To be the church is to belong to a group where the walls that divide humans have already been taken down. 'For he [Christ] himself is our peace, who has made the two groups one and has destroyed the barrier, the dividing wall of hostility' (Eph. 2:14). And then in Galatians 3:28: 'There is neither Jew nor Gentile, neither slave nor free, nor is there male and female, for you are all one in Christ Jesus.'

The church of Christ is already a movement with a solid basis to overcome prejudice and bigotry. And that's why the church has pursued social reform throughout its history. And in areas where we have failed in this, we must hold up our hands and confess it!

While heeding the dangers of politicism on the progressive side, the church must also be wary of the pitfalls of aligning uncritically with the reactionary conservatives. For starters, why should we expect the secular world to live by the morality we espouse? Harking back to a golden age, it is easy to overlook that our culture is now post-Christian. So why would unbelievers take on the moral norms we adhere to? They are not pretending to be Christians, and it's unreasonable to expect them to behave in that way. Why should they wait until marriage before they share a bed? Why would they stay celibate when they are attracted to someone of the same sex? Why would they pass laws we say are 'biblical'? It is absurd to blame an unbeliever for being an unbeliever, and our judgments against them lack credibility. We need to hear from Paul, who never taught that it was our business to judge unbelievers. 'What business is it of mine to judge those outside the church? Are you not to judge those inside?' (1 Cor. 5:12). His concern was to put our own house in order.

Destructive allegiances

Another danger that comes with uncritically aligning with the political right is where it might land us. Those who side with reactionary conservativism are likely to get caught up in the backlash. As the cultural and political gulf widens, a growing extremism is likely to be the outcome. This is something conservatives could easily be swept up in.

The twentieth century has a sobering historical lesson to instruct us here. In the 1920s, Catholic and Protestant churches in Germany were caught up in a conservative reaction against social and political changes that were occurring then. This included the growth of the communist movement. It is striking that leading orthodox theologians openly supported the Nazi regime in its early phase. For them, and for Christian conservatives today, C. S. Lewis expresses the danger: '. . . your extra dislike of the one error to draw you gradually into the opposite one'.[11]

Forgetting to be salt and light

When the church politicizes, it loses sight of what it means for us to be salt and light. We don't achieve this by hitching ourselves to a political cause. Our salt and light function comes through having the mark of Christ's distinctive character in our lives.

Belonging to Christ and reflecting him is the way this happens. Here is the path to a deeper transformation – on the inside. The transformation begins with us, an interior transformation that has nothing to do with the political. Any change we make to culture begins from this place.

---

11 C. S. Lewis, *Mere Christianity* (New York: HarperOne, 2001), p. 186.

The treatment – living under Christ's Lordship over all of life

We say Jesus is Lord over our lives, but is he, and how far will we allow his authority to govern our affairs? Are we prepared to bow to him in all things – even when this is uncomfortable and against the grain of what the world stands for?

The only Ruler

To cure us of our disordered allegiance, we must see and acknowledge Christ's total Lordship. As Paul says in 1 Timothy 6:15, he is 'the only Ruler'. His throne is in heaven, giving him a rule that encompasses all things – including the social and political order. Christ's authority to rule is conferred by his Father who 'gave him the name above every name, that at the name of Jesus every knee should bow' (Phil. 2:9–10). Every believer should be in awe of the sheer scope of Christ's authority. He has the power not because of a democratic majority, but because his Father has granted him this role.

The weight of acknowledging Christ's full Lordship is that it gives Christians the broader vision. Going well beyond the political, Christ's rule over us extends into every area of life. It affects family, our work life, how we engage our neighbours and the litter on our streets. Jesus' Lordship is nothing less than an all-of-life allegiance. There is no area of our life and experience of which he is not Lord.

The wonderful thing about being a Christian is living meaningfully under this broader vision. Such a perspective puts politicism in its proper context. While this realm may look and feel big, it's actually a reduced perspective on reality. Letting Christ be Lord is what opens us up to the larger vision.

Nothing less than a total allegiance

As Jesus is the one who is rightfully Lord, we are called to a quality of allegiance that is nothing less than complete loyalty to him. He is worthy of this, having purchased us with something more valuable than we can ever know – his own blood shed on the cross. The Son of God laid down his life for us. That means bearing reproach for his sake is entirely acceptable because he did the same for us when executed by the Romans.

When the cross is central to our vision, we have a motivation to stand firm, even when a buffeting comes. We owe him everything – and that includes standing firm when enduring public flak for bearing the name 'Christian'.

No place for accommodation

Given the cultural opposition we face as Christians, the temptation to a disordered allegiance is real. That makes accommodation a tangible danger. Francis Schaeffer warned of this very thing:

> In the case of an accommodating evangelicalism, there has been a tendency to talk about a wider, richer Christianity and to become more deeply involved in culture, but at the same time to accommodate to the world spirit about us at each crucial point. Note that the result is then the same. Despite claims of cultural relevance, an accommodating evangelicalism also leaves the destructive surrounding culture increasingly unchallenged.[12]

Only with a strong allegiance to Jesus can we resist. It is reminiscent of the golden image incident recorded in Daniel 3. King Nebuchadnezzar sets up a ninety-foot-tall golden statue in Babylon's capital's public square. Imagine this as Nelson's Column in Trafalgar Square in London, or something comparable in Times Square in New York. With the full force of state law behind it, everyone is ordered to bow down as a test of allegiance to the new moral order. Any who remain

---

12 *The Complete Works of Francis A. Schaeffer: A Christian Worldview* (Wheaton: Crossway Books, 1985), p. 425.

on their feet will stand out in the most obvious manner and be subject to punishment. That was what Shadrach, Meshach and Abednego did. They stayed on their feet because their allegiance held firm to God.

Will we bow before the golden image of politicism, or will we stay faithful to Christ in all things?

A better identity

Our allegiance to Christ will strengthen as our core identity is rooted in him. As we saw earlier, many today find theirs in identity politics. Some are identifying themselves in the various letters that make up LGBTQ+. On the other side, people are identifying themselves (again) by their nationality and race. How Christians root their identity will determine how they stand when the storm comes. We must commit to the identity that Christ alone confers as we bow to his Lordship. Being 'in Christ' stretches beyond our political allegiances, our national ones and our sexual ones. Our primary identity lies in the Lord who reigns over all things.

Right priorities

Our total allegiance to Christ's Lordship also frees us from having to make an either/or choice in the current political climate. To bow to Christ is not the same as choosing for the politically progressive or conservative. Under his rule we can be thoughtful and challenge both the left and the right in different ways and on different points. Tim Keller helpfully points out that there are lots of 'political' matters where the Bible 'does not give exact answers to these questions for every time, place and culture'.[13] How to solve the problems of economics and climate change are cases of this. Such matters call for the insight of wisdom to make a good judgment. And because there isn't

---

13 Timothy Keller, 'How Do Christians Fit into the Two-Party System? They Don't', *The New York Times*, 29 September 2018, <nytimes.com/2018/09/29/opinion/sunday/christians-politics-belief.html>.

a clear biblical mandate, we must be open to viewpoints that take a different position.

It is possible to stand above the political fray and think clearly because our allegiance to Christ roots us in a place that transcends the political. Belonging to him means we are residents of Augustine's two cities – the City of Man and the City of God.[14] Christ rules both, but he calls his people to a higher loyalty to the City of God. Staying true to this loyalty helps shape how we engage with the other city – the political one. There are moments that open for Christians to engage with the *polis*. When this happens, significant social trans-formations may occur from the top down as the church uses its influence to make for better goodness and justice within the social order.

At other historic moments, this door closes, and belonging to the City of God calls us to step back. Then is our time for being a faithful presence. We engage with our mission in a quieter manner – by loving our immediate neighbours. In such moments, the church would do well to heed Paul's instruction:

> Now about your love for one another we do not need to write to you, for you yourselves have been taught by God to love each other. And in fact, you do love all of God's family throughout Macedonia. Yet we urge you, brothers and sisters, to do so more and more, and to make it your ambition to lead a quiet life: you should mind your own business and work with your hands, just as we told you, so that your daily life may win the respect of outsiders.
>
> (1 Thess. 4:9–12)

Lead a quiet life! What does that look like? It's living the good life Christ calls us to – the life of love. There is something so admirable

---

14 This idea is developed in Augustine of Hippo's book *The City of God*, written in AD 426.

in this that it wins the respect of unbelievers. And what stands out about this good life isn't trying to take over the world by joining the right political cause. No, it's working with our hands. It's about daily life! A life for the good of our local communities.

As a minority, the first Christians couldn't dream of gaining control of state powers. They played their role by being little Christs to the social realities that confronted them. Here was an empire that didn't protect widows and abandoned its orphans. Early Christians stepped in to do what the state failed to do – the Christlike act of love for actual people in need. This was the subversive fulfilment that marked them. Today we need to recover the same practical love in our local neighbourhoods.

No place for an ugly orthodoxy

As we remain faithful to Christ, we must also resist being lured into an ugly orthodoxy. The rule we have bowed to is based on the inherent power and goodness of the one who holds it. These are attributes we have already examined in chapter 3 and chapter 5. These two characteristics make him fit to rule. His authority over all things was not something he gained in a power play. And that means there is nothing tyrannical and oppressive in how he exercises it. The progressives are right to suspect how power is abused, but at the end of the day someone must exercise it. Whereas every human power structure has an inbuilt bias and injustice, the authority Christ wields is good and just. And that's why his power is also an expression of his perfect goodness.

Our engagement with the world around us must reflect his good rule. That means there is no place for an ugly orthodoxy. Rather, we must speak 'the truth in love' (Eph. 4:15). When unbelievers oppose us, we don't stop loving them, because Christ commits us to a higher standard. No profiling – except as the image of God. No grievance and outrage because the final judgment belongs to Christ. We will speak with a voice that is not belligerent but is filled with clarity and discernment. Jesus as the friend of sinners will be our example in terms of a response. Because of what he models, we can extend genuine love and welcome to our enemies.

Marginalization – setback or opportunity?

With Christianity becoming increasingly marginalized in public, it's worth asking whether this is a setback or an opportunity. With the likelihood of increasing levels of hostility, will this be to our detriment or our benefit? If being battered makes us more committed to following Jesus in all things, it can only work for our good. Now is our opportunity to learn 'a long obedience in the same direction'.[15] This flows from an undivided allegiance and obedience to Christ, no matter what the cost.

Jesus was clear in John 15 that our allegiance to him would lead to the world hating us. And this animosity has the potential to refine our love for Christ. To suffer a rejection for his name's sake is something generations of believers have had to endure. It is part of what a commitment to him entails. As Jesus 'learned obedience from what he suffered' (Hebrews 5:8), so will we.

If the public pressure on Christians continues to rise – which is likely – it presents us with a choice. Public intimidation has always been a test for the believers' allegiance. Experiencing this often serves to strengthen it. When it is fashionable to be a Christian, there is little cost to following Jesus. When it is unfashionable, the cost of discipleship is the either/or choice our culture places on us.

And when the church knows Christ as Lord, we don't become anxious as things fall apart. He is the One who has promised to make all things right. It's not our job to save the world – Christ alone has what it takes for that. Knowing this allows us to live from the place of rest, even in the middle of the tumult and noise of the culture wars.

---

15 Title of book by Eugene Peterson (Illinois: IVP, 2021).

Chapter summary

*Politicism is a cultural ideal believing that political factors are the dominant means to redeeming this world from its problems. Being overly concerned with 'relevance', the church's engagement with culture has been hijacked by the political issues of our day. Under a growing hostility from the new moral order, the church feels pressured to join forces with either the radical progressives or the reactionary conservatives. This has led to a **disordered allegiance** and a corresponding failure to appreciate how Christ's kingdom works as salt and light. To overcome this aspect of our worldliness, we must recover the knowledge of Christ's Lordship over all of life. Bowing to his rule in all things frees us to be a good and vital force for transforming society. A total allegiance to Christ's rule will help us stay true, even when we are persecuted for his name's sake. It will also free us to stay loving towards those who hate us.*

Questions

- On matters like sex and gender, whose judgment do you think matters most to you – our culture's or Christ's?
- Do you feel equipped to deal with the fast pace of moral change in our society today? If not, what can you do to change this? And how can the church help the next generation face the challenges?
- If the persecution of Christians were to intensify significantly, how do you think you would fare? How can the church better model Christlike love and service to our immediate neighbours, even if we are increasingly marginalized?

Further reading

Os Guinness, *Prophetic Untimeliness: A Challenge to the Idol of Relevance* (Michigan: Baker, 2005).

David T. Koyzis, *Political Visions and Illusions: A Survey and Christian Critique of Contemporary Ideologies* (Illinois: IVP Academic, 2003).

Patrick Deneen, *Why Liberalism Failed* (Yale: Yale University Press, 2018).

James Davison Hunter, *To Change the World: The Irony, Tragedy, and Possibility of Christianity in the Late Modern World* (Oxford: Oxford University Press, 2010).

Vern S. Poythress, *The Lordship of Christ: Serving Our Savior All of the Time, in All of Life, with All of Our Heart* (Wheaton, Ill.: Crossway, 2016).

7

Where do we go from here?

> Christianity has died many times and risen again;
> for it had a God who knew the way out of the grave.
> (G. K. Chesterton)[1]

The ground we have covered in this book does not have the feel-good factor our culture craves. We have had to confront a big negative, namely a church disordered by its worldliness. We have let other things eclipse Christ at the centre, leading to a disordered trust, a disordered vision, a disordered affection and a disordered allegiance. The super-values that shape our culture have influenced the church and we are quickly becoming secular.

What can the righteous do?

The urgency of the situation calls for some serious soul searching. In Psalm 11 we read a lament written when the nation of Israel was in a terrible crisis. Something dreadful was happening, making it feel as if things were falling apart. Out of this calamity, verse 3 posed the critical question, 'When the foundations are being destroyed, what can the righteous do?' I cannot think of a more important question for us to grapple with today.

We are living in a moment well described by a line in a famous war poem by William Butler Yeats: 'things fall apart; the centre cannot hold'.[2] Clearly the foundations of the Secular Age are shaking. But so are the foundations of the contemporary church. They are

---

1   G. K. Chesterton, *The Everlasting Man* (London: Burns & Oates, 1974), p. 249.
2   William Butler Yeats (1865–1939), 'The Second Coming' (public domain).

systemically being eroded by our worldliness. As we conform to the Secular Age, it has triggered a series of waves that wash up on our shores. We are in danger of being swept away.

So what can the righteous do? The following verse in Psalm 11 poses the solution in seeing that:

> The LORD is in his holy temple;
> The LORD is on his heavenly throne.
> He observes everyone on earth;
> his eyes examine them.
> (Ps. 11:4)

The answer to our crisis is simple – indeed, it couldn't be more straightforward.

The simplicity of the solution may leave readers unimpressed. Diagnosing the problem of the world in the church is no simple matter – just as reading this book may have taxed you. Our tendency is to think that complex problems require complex solutions. But in terms of what the righteous can do, the solution is straightforward: Jesus must be smuggled back into the church. That will make the decisive difference.

This resolution to our crisis is itself a subversion of our activist tendencies. Like modernists, Christians like to approach problems with a technical eye. Such tactics look for structural fixes to challenging predicaments. I know this is my default for problem solving.

Years ago, on a bus near the North Korean border, a group of us were discussing the crisis of the contemporary church and what we could do to reform it. My contribution proposed a revolutionary overhaul from the ground up. That pressed the buttons of my thoughtful fellow travellers, who pushed me to say more. I replied that we needed something on the scale of the Benedictine movement. The church should commit itself to becoming a radically different kind of community – a counter-order in the world to show the better way. We can only challenge the behemoth of modernity with something that is revolutionary on the plane of the sociological.

I was feeling pleased with my call to arms when someone across the aisle said, 'Hmm, sounds a lot like a revolution that doesn't need Christ.'

That retort stunned me, because it was true. Any fix for the church that doesn't require Christ as its solution is only another form of being worldly.

Many today can see the problems, and there is no shortage of resolutions for a struggling church. One recent example is Rod Dreher's *Benedict Option*,[3] calling for Christians to safeguard themselves from a modernity that so radically undermines their distinctiveness.

Over the past fifty years the church has invested much in addressing the malaises of the contemporary church. Many of our initiatives have been beneficial. In the interests of singing a new song to the Lord, we found fresh forms of worship to bring it up to date. This has been a good thing. Using the common vernacular is crucial and, after all, why should the devil have all the best tunes? Of course, if we follow the latest cultural tastes in music, we will soon find it becomes outdated. I recently attended a church that had been groundbreaking in its music at the turn of the millennium. Twenty years later it sounded old and behind the times. Younger Christians were looking elsewhere for something more suitable to their tastes.

We have also played with various models for doing church. Our social context is complex in the way it divides our time and loyalties. Church leaders have been concerned about how to create a stronger sense of our community as the people of God. In the late 1980s, cell churches became popular. Cells are the biological life sources in our bodies, so why not create cell groups (or home groups or community groups, or other similar names) to do the same for the church? As a

---

3 Rod Dreher, *The Benedict Option: A Strategy for Christians in a Post-Christian Nation* (New York: Sentinel, 2017).

way of organizing our life together, these have been invaluable and a good reform.

Through the 1990s and early 2000s we saw the rise of the emergent church. A disillusionment with old forms of the institutional church made people long for something new. This movement was trying to get beyond the labelling. It wanted to transcend being theologically 'conservative' or 'liberal'. In the end it created enough labels to rival some of the biggest online sellers – post-evangelical, post-liberal, neo-evangelical, neo-charismatic, and so on. Despite all the hype and promise, it has pretty much disappeared. Ironically, many of its leaders have turned themselves into self-help gurus copying some of the more worldly aspects of evangelicalism!

So, over recent decades there have been good reforms – and some not so good. We have often opted for novelty – as if something fresh would undoubtedly be good for us. What we can also assert is that none of our reforms has prevented us from becoming worldly. Only Jesus can do that.

It may be bad, but we have been here before

The simplicity of the way out of worldliness should keep us from despair as we face our present crisis. Looking back throughout our long history, we see the church has been here before. Every time its foundations were being destroyed, the restoration factor was the same: seeing the Lord in his holy temple and the Lord on his heavenly throne.

A striking parallel with our times is the eighteenth century. The Industrial Revolution created social upheaval. People flocked to the cities for job opportunities in the new factories, but because machines were replacing human labour, the result was misery for the masses. It wasn't a moment for human flourishing, and a moral decline shook the British Isles. A roaring gin trade drove many to drink to compensate for the misery, and alcoholism rocketed.

There was also a degradation in cultural entertainment. Cock-fighting became popular, and so was a form of the bullfight, when a terrified beast would be chained to a post with trained dogs to savage it. Public executions of criminals were like an outing to the cinema, and spectators would buy tickets to watch a hanging. Porno-graphic literature was popular, devoured without shame in the pubs and coffee houses of London. There was also a roaring trade in cross-dressing rent boys, and market stalls in Covent Garden sold contraceptives. Here was another hedonistic age promoted by a group called the Libertines. They committed themselves to a lifestyle of pleasure that encouraged men to assert their sexual dominance over women. It was a time of banality when the masses lost their sensitivity to higher meanings. Thomas Carlyle – a public intellectual of the day – was renowned for his satirical descriptions of the age. One went like this: 'Stomach well alive, soul extinct.'[4]

The state of the church matched the state of the culture. An enculturation had occurred, leaving it in a low-ebb moment. This accommodation was to some key ideas that were dominant in the eighteenth century. Among the intellectual elites was a new commit-ment to human reason. Faith was viewed as something that fell short of reason. Philosophy shaped churches more than the Bible did. William Blackstone attended the best churches in London and said he 'did not hear a single discourse which had more Christianity in it than the writings of Cicero'.[5] As the authority of the Bible was eclipsed, so was Christ. It led to a new morality centred on doing your duty to the Crown and the state rather than an obedience to Christ.

John Wesley was set in the middle of this malaise. After theo-logical training at Oxford, he was ordained into the Anglican

---

4 Quoted by Wesley J. Bready in *England Before and After Wesley: The Evangelical Revival and Social Reform* (London: Hodder & Stoughton, 1938), p. 40.
5 Quoted in *The Twentieth Century* (United Kingdom: Twentieth Century Limited, 1879), p. 284.

Church. Wesley knew something was wrong and joined a 'holy club' for a more serious pursuit of the Christian life. Here was an equivalent of the emergent church – something new to challenge the old institution. It was when he encountered another fringe group called the Moravians that everything changed. On 24 May 1738 he had an experience when he felt his 'heart strangely warmed'.[6] In this moment he encountered the living Christ, and it changed everything.

Wesley's faith was radicalized in the best way, setting into motion a remarkable movement called the Great Awakening. It was a time when Christians woke up and saw Christ. Because the established church was resistant to the message of the Great Awakening, John Wesley devoted his life to open-air preaching. With simplicity and passion, he proclaimed a vision of Christ and his gospel. Priests tried to keep parishioners away, but they turned out in their thousands. It was a time of renewal for believers who had their own hearts 'strangely warmed', and many nominal believers were truly converted.

The transformation for the church was groundbreaking – and so was the social impact. It led to reforms in education and health provision. Initiatives in orphan care, book publishing and a host of other matters swept the culture.[7] Even secular historians acknowledge how much good the Great Awakening accomplished. Many believe it prevented England from sliding into the chaos of revolution that marked France. What it showed is that when a worldly church is reawakened to Christ, it makes all the difference – first to the church and then, as a by-product, to society. The Wesleyan revolution helped shape the church so it became the salt and light of the world, rather than the world being the salt and light of the church.

We need another awakening like this – one that restores Christ to his rightful place in the church so we become little Christs in the

---

6 John and Charles Wesley, *Selected Prayers, Hymns, Journal Notes, Sermons, Letters and Treatises* (United States: Paulist Press, 1981), p. 107.

7 Ian J. Shaw explores this in his book *Lessons from Old Masters on Evangelicals and Social Action: From John Wesley to John Stott* (London: IVP, 2021).

world. Andrew Murray appreciated what this would bring: a radical renewal of the church, 'casting out the spirit of worldliness and selfishness, and making God and His love triumph in the heart and life'.[8]

The two-legged church – reformation and revival

For Jesus to become the centre of his church, two things are required. To ask, 'What can the righteous do?' will require the church to stand on two legs. One is reformation and the other is revival, and both are necessary.

Reformation is what we do to put the affairs of the church in order. What has been deformed by the world needs reforming. Protestants sometimes believe there has only been one reformation in our history – the one that occurred in the sixteenth century. The great reformers of that time were clear in their understanding that this kind of reformation was something the church should constantly engage in. They coined the term *semper reformanda*, which is Latin for 'the church must always be reformed'. There have been many reformations, and each is a tale of how a few turned the church upside down.

Revivals happen when Christ steps in to put his temple in order. When the church is in a state of collapse, only the Lord can intervene. Revival is a 'mouth-to-mouth' resuscitation – Christ coming to the rescue to breathe life into his bride who has stopped breathing and is acutely ill.

If my diagnosis is correct, then I believe we have reached such a moment – we need divine resuscitation. Christ does this through a special operation of his Spirit. When revivals occur, no one doubts that the Holy Spirit is working. These come with a divine power that

---

8 'Andrew Murray 1828–1917)', The Jesus Gathering, <www.thejesusgathering.org/andrew-murray.html>.

is irresistible. Revival is the dramatic intervention of the Triune God to revitalize the church.

Looking back on the history of the church, we see the effects of these revivals. At moments when the church was in terrible decay, great reversals happened. And that's what revival is – a great reversal. There is no formula for revival, and the church cannot manufacture it. It is enough to know that Christ did something dramatic – at the right time and in the right way.

When revivals have occurred, they have made all the difference. And whenever revivals have happened, there have been decisive benefits to nations and cultures. When the church is revitalized, there is an overflow to the world. With Christ's glory and weight in his church, it could not be otherwise. That is why revival is accompanied by lots of conversions as Christ's gospel has a new power to save.

Because revivals are beyond our strategies and techniques, all we can do is cry out to the Lord for one. In his Word he encourages this with a promise:

> If my people, who are called by my name, will humble themselves and pray and seek my face and turn from their wicked ways, then I will hear from heaven, and I will forgive their sin and will heal their land.
>
> (2 Chr. 7:14)

The point to grasp is that when the church becomes worldly, we need both reformation and revival. To attempt reformation without revival is not enough because it leaves the matter of resuscitation in our hands. If you have collapsed in a fast-food outlet with a terrible pain in your chest, you cannot do CPR on yourself. You need someone to come to your rescue, someone who knows what they're doing – thirty chest compressions followed by two rescue breaths into your airways. That is where revival as Christ's intervention is necessary. However, to hold only to revival becomes its own problem. It can turn into a passivism where we wring our hands in despair at how awful everything is, and do nothing to prepare ourselves.

I was converted in a church that was influenced by Dr Martyn Lloyd-Jones. He was pastor of Westminster Chapel in London and a light for the evangelical church through much of the twentieth century. A typical Sunday sermon was full of rich theology, with the Puritans as a guiding light. And the influence of Lloyd-Jones schooled me in the history of revivals. They were the beacon of hope for our hour, and we prayed for something like that to happen. However, because revival was our only hope, we could do nothing but wait for it, and that led to an unhelpful passivism. It also created a counsel of despair. It felt like a scene from Samuel Beckett's play *Waiting for Godot*. The two main characters are told to wait by a tree for Godot to show up. What is not clear is when and how Godot will do that. That leaves them in confusion and doubt. As bad as things are, the church must not become inactive as we look to the Lord to help us.

After some years in these circles, reading Francis Schaeffer (the pastor, philosopher and apologist best known for starting L'Abri Fellowship in Switzerland) was a game changer for me. Through him I discovered a reformation tradition that combines the historic faith and the modern world. Matters such as education, politics, psychology, the arts and a Christian philosophical viewpoint widened the scope of Christ's Lordship.

As I engaged with this new reformational heritage, I inadvertently left my revival roots behind. Recently I have embraced them again. Given how worldly the church has become, revival is a necessity. There comes a point when the church is so impotent, we can only look to Christ for a refresh. But that does not mean we just sit and wait. If the temple has become a ruin, we have work to do – and that is what reformation is for.

A reforming church

What will it look like for the church to engage in reformation? There is an Old Testament incident that provides a starting point. In the seventh century BC the temple in Jerusalem was in ruins. A young king named Josiah stumped up the funds for the rebuilding project, but prior to that some rubble removal was necessary. This rubble was in the form of idols. 2 Kings chapter 22 and 23 record:

> The king ordered Hilkiah the high priest, the priests next in rank and the doorkeepers to remove from the temple of the LORD all the articles made for Baal and Asherah and all the starry hosts. He burned them outside Jerusalem in the fields of the Kidron Valley and took the ashes to Bethel.
> (2 Kgs 23:4)

A bit later in the chapter:

> He pulled down the altars the kings of Judah had erected on the roof near the upper room of Ahaz, and the altars Manasseh had built in the two courts of the temple of the LORD. He removed them from there, smashed them to pieces and threw the rubble into the Kidron Valley.
> (2 Kgs 23:12)

Reformation in the church always requires rubble removal, and this rubble will look different depending on time and place. Back in the sixteenth century it existed as political and economic corruption inside the Catholic Church. It had an infrastructure that made those at the top fabulously rich. Often the position of a bishop or a cardinal went to the highest bidder. This wealth was at the expense of the poor who were terribly exploited. One way they were manipulated was through the selling of indulgences. The initial part of Luther's reform was to clear out this rubble. He did this by exposing how ungodly such practices were.

Reformation for the church today must begin with a 'clear-out'. To reform well, the church needs to know what has gone wrong. It requires clear insight into the way the foundations are being destroyed. For us, that means understanding how we are worldly. We have seen that becoming worldly can go undetected. It's like the unseen yeast in a batch of bread dough or a virus particle so small we can only measure it in nanometres.

But with the right discernment, 'the world' need not stay hidden. It is possible to detect how the foundations are being eroded – an exposure of how 'the world' is infiltrating. Thankfully, the Lord has gifted his church with people who have done excellent work in diagnosing the problem. Over the past hundred years, there have been modern-day prophets who understand the times and have seen how the church is accommodating. People like G. K. Chesterton, Dorothy L. Sayers, C. S. Lewis, Francis Schaeffer, Os Guinness and others have done the hard work – to name but a few. With their help, the church can be equipped to look at the foundations and see what is wrong.

Back to basics

We should be clear that a cultural engagement to see the problem does not go far enough. On its own, a cultural critique is only rubble removal and stops short of affirmative reform. What has not been so forthcoming in our day are positive applications for what reform looks like. And so the question remains, 'What can the righteous do?'

Once again, this involves nothing novel. It is going back to basics. The idea of *re-forming* is about restoring what has been lost. It is a return to something. For Luther it was a return to the simplicity of the New Testament. The magisterium of the Catholic Church had obscured the basics and hence Luther saw the necessity of recovering justification by faith. This for him was a doctrine by which the church either stands or falls.

Reformation is never about innovation, but shoring up the foundations Christ has already given his church to build on.

Back to the Bible

Strengthening the things that remain means first giving the Bible a central place in the church's life. We are founded on a Word that is received and passed on from one generation to another. Periodically the church loses its grip on this Word, and this is ruinous for the cause.

When King Josiah was conducting his reform, it was Hilkiah who discovered a scroll in some dusty corner of the temple. When it became clear that this was the Book of the Law, it mortified the young king. He made sure they read this Word of the Lord to the people. It was a back-to-basics moment. We are told in 2 Chronicles 34:14–33 that it affected the Israelites, making them return to the Lord. That is reformation.

Our back-to-basics today must allow for a fresh airing of the Bible. This involves engaging with Scripture as a living Word. The theologian John Webster contends:

> One of the offices of Holy Scripture in the life of the church is to service this divine directive by giving voice to its inescapable presence. Holy Scripture is one of the points at which the assembly is laid open to the sheer otherness of the divine word.[9]

The Bible is not a book of dead facts making for boring sermons. When reduced to facts, our expositions follow a clichéd and predictable line of enquiry. To be reformed, we need an address that breaks up our ordinary ways of perceiving. The Bible as a living speech act of Christ does that. His Word is not just facts about him; they are Words directly from him, addressed to his people. That

---

9   John Webster, *Holy Scripture: A Dogmatic Sketch* (Cambridge: Cambridge University Press, 2003), p. 51.

makes Scripture a dynamic communication, and getting back to basics means letting him speak. Doing that moves us beyond the pre-packaged EA (easy answers) sermons provided by many preachers today. They package their talks so neatly that there's no thought of spurring the listener on to go away and do some mining for themselves.

When the Bible is to us the living Word of Christ, we don't just mine it for answers. Now we allow it to question us. To be questioned is to be unsettled and moved from our comfort zones. It awakens something within us and directs us to a richer horizon. Because this Word lives and breathes with something personal and life-giving, it engages the heart as well as the head. Analogous to what great art does, the living Word engages the imagination, opening the eye of faith to see further. Breaking up our customary (and worldly) way of viewing things, we are now beyond inertia and coming to new life.

Part of the wake-up factor of the living Word is that it breaks through the seduction of worldliness. Paul says as much in 2 Corinthians 10 when he refers to the mind of Christ with the power to demolish strongholds (vv. 4–5). Before its brilliant light we can see through the pretensions. Here is a power to resist being enculturated and conformed. That makes it a transformational Word. Paul again in Romans 12:2: 'Do not conform to the pattern of this world, but be transformed by the renewing of your mind. Then you will be able to test and approve what God's will is – his good, pleasing and perfect will.' That is the power of the Bible when we let it out of the cage.

Back to the church's confession

Another key aspect of going back to basics is taking our stand on the church's confession. By that I mean beliefs the church has held as central through its long history and tradition. Why do I add this as an essential? Isn't the Bible enough?

Many Christians have forgotten the rich inheritance of the church. We have received a faith tradition handed down to us – one that is alive. Jaroslav Pelikan reminded us that 'tradition is the living faith of the dead; traditionalism is the dead faith of the living'.[10] To strengthen the things that remain, we must take our historic faith seriously. This stretches back to the early centuries of the church, when various creeds were formulated, setting the parameters on what was considered orthodox. Later, confessions were compiled, outlining the more detailed commitments of a particular denomination or tradition. Some were Reformed (the Westminster Confession of Faith) alongside other church traditions (Lutheran, Wesleyan and so on).

Wherever our church is situated, it is beneficial to be aware of and respectful of our roots. Both creeds and confessions were put together by great theologians who absorbed the Bible into their consciousness and thought Christ's thoughts after him. Under the Holy Spirit's guidance, these have helped the church to remain orthodox.

Today, this legacy is largely ignored, and to our detriment. Many Christians are hardly aware of these historical foundations. Many like to think that we have arrived at the basics because of our commitment to Scripture alone. I once sat with a group of independents who were planting a church. They started with the all-important issue of what beliefs would define them as a congregation. They divided a whiteboard into two columns of primary and secondary doctrine. There was a call for people to shout out what they thought were primary and secondary beliefs based on the Bible. I could not believe what I was hearing. There was no mention of the great creeds and confessions of the church, developed through scholarly toil and rigorous criticism. It was a Bible-only 'let's figure it out'. I'm reminded of what Goethe said about philosophy: 'He who cannot draw on three thousand years is living from hand to mouth.'[11] The same is true of two thousand years of church history! Because of that we don't have to live from hand to mouth but can make use of a rich resource.

---

10 In an interview in *U.S. News & World Report*, 26 July 1989.
11 Johann Wolfgang von Goethe, *West-östlicher Divan*, section 5, 'Buch des Unmuts' (Berlin: Matthes & Seitz, 2016).

A pragmatic approach to church – the 'what works is what's good' approach – makes the historic faith fade out. Such concerns seem irrelevant to growing the church in the modern age. For a host of reasons, we have lost the church's confession. Our reform must involve engaging with it seriously once more. It is a fundamental we must recover. As the cultural buffeting ratchets up, this will be an essential if we are to stand firm. The early church was a doctrinally bounded movement that fearlessly confessed its faith – even in the middle of persecution. The confessional aspect was an important part of why it stood firm in its allegiance to Jesus.

Recovering the church's confession will also end our love affair with theological novelty. Over the last century, the church has felt the need to be doctrinally progressive. Rather than taking our stand on the faith once received, we thought we could come up with something better. Returning to our roots, we see we do not need inventiveness. We just need to be faithful to a body of teaching once delivered to the saints that began with Christ's apostles. Keeping the faith means standing in our inheritance. *Semper reformanda* is about always returning to orthodoxy rather than a progressive evolution!

Reforming our worship

The church exists to exalt Christ. When the Covid lockdown closed the doors of our churches in 2020, the most devastating impact was not being able to worship Christ together. For me, this ripped out the heart of the church because this is what we are – a people who live in praise of Christ. Our vibrancy and health depend on the quality of our worship. It is another basic that defines us.

Attempts to reform the church today must address this aspect of our corporate life. It was key to what happened in the sixteenth-century Reformation. The Catholic Church was conducting its worship in Latin. Because only clergymen spoke this ancient language, the church's worship was unintelligible to the masses. That necessitated a 'make it relevant' approach. Back then it was as simple as ensuring a worship service was in the vernacular of the people. German hymns for German Christians, English for the English. It was a revolutionary move.

No doubt our reform must focus here too. Today, worship is a contentious matter, often coming down to style and form. This can bog us down, so we miss the point. Unlike the sixteenth-century Reformation, I don't believe relevance is where reform is needed. We have already invested plenty in ensuring our language is up to date. Our reform requires a different focus – call it a 'reverence over relevance' approach. We must ask, is our corporate worship worthy of the Christ we adore? And what would Christ say if he were to sit at the back and observe our worship time?

I am not advocating that the church should throw out the drum kit and go back to exclusive psalmody. But we need to consider more than pragmatism, and ask whether the medium for our worship is fitting for who Christ is. I believe worship today is often more weighted towards Jesus our friend than to Christ the Lord in his transcendent splendour.

Reforming our fellowship

Another basic to our reforming activity is to strengthen the quality of our life together. Church is not a set of activities – programmes, causes, communication and outreach. We are a living body of people who are bound to Christ and each other. Our relationship to him includes our relationship to each other. Community must be front and centre because Christ is. That makes the church a living fellowship that is profoundly relational. This feature is so integral to what the church is that Francis Schaeffer called it an 'orthodoxy of community':

> But one cannot explain the explosive dynamite, the dunamis,
> of the early church apart from the fact that they practiced two
> things simultaneously: orthodoxy of doctrine and orthodoxy

of community in the midst of the visible church, a community which the world could see. By the grace of God, therefore, the church must be known simultaneously for its purity of doctrine and the reality of its community. Our churches have so often been only preaching points with very little emphasis on community. But exhibition of the love of God in practice is beautiful and must be there.[12]

Our activist focus on programmes and causes often creates conditions that are not conducive to being a loving community. Church is something you do rather than a fellowship to take part in. I hear many Christians cite the lack of community as a significant factor in their disaffection. That is why I believe the reality of community in our churches requires a renewed focus. Indeed, to give this our attention might be the key to a significant reformation in the church today. If the quality of our fellowship were to set the agenda, this would rearrange our priorities. A lot of what makes up church life could fall by the wayside. Our e-bulletins advertising all our church activities might become redundant.

The quality of our community will be essential as the tide of opposition increases from our culture. It will be key to our holding fast. Being a close-knit community was an important aspect of what enabled the early church to withstand persecution. Facing reproach when you have the support and comfort of a community that believes in what you do makes it bearable.

A loving community is also essential to making church attractive in the Secular Age. Such was the kinship of the early Christians that those outside remarked on the love they had for each other. Our culture has created conditions for fragmenting community. People live behind walls that isolate them from others. Digital community is one revolution of our time where the bulk of our connection with

---

12 Francis A. Schaeffer, *The Complete Works of Francis A. Schaeffer: Volume 4, A Christian View of the Church* (Wheaton, Ill.: Crossway, 1985), p. 152.

others is online. The quality of actual community in the church goes much further. I believe people are hungry for this even if they do not know it. Now is when genuine community can have a revolutionary impact.

In his customary pithy way, Blaise Pascal encourages Christians to live in a reality that is so attractive people will wish it were true:

> Men despise religion. They hate it and are afraid it may be true. The cure for this is first to ensure that religion is not contrary to reason but worthy of reverence and respect. Next make it attractive, make good men wish it were true, and then show that it is.[13]

I believe a church fellowship living out the reality of loving relationships will be the attraction factor. While others deride what we believe, they will long for the life we share. Francis Schaeffer believed the world had 'a right to judge whether we are Christians and whether the Father sent the Son, on the basis of observable love shown among all true Christians'.[14] This love was, for Schaeffer, 'the mark of the Christian'.[15] Our reform must create the conditions that demonstrate this. This back-to-basics is not something requiring high-level organization. There is no programme for a loving community. It is a reality to be lived.

Living as a cross-wise people

Strengthening the things that remain also involves being a cross-wise people. Christ crucified is the foundation of his church, and any reform we engage with must centre on this.

---

13 Blaise Pascal, *Pensées*, translated by A. J. Krailsheimer (London: Penguin, 1994), p. 4.
14 Schaeffer, *The Complete Works*, p. 33.
15 Title of book by Francis A. Schaeffer, *The Mark of the Christian* (Illinois: IVP, 2006).

For centuries the church has made the cross its defining symbol to show this. Christians hang them in churches, wear them as jewellery and tattoo them on their skin. But what does the cross symbolize? For Paul it represented a reality that made the church an unworldly people: 'May I never boast except in the cross of our Lord Jesus Christ, through which the world has been crucified to me, and I to the world' (Gal. 6:14). He reflects here that something about the cross kills the world in the believer. And that is what crucifixion is – an instrument for carrying out the death penalty. At an incalculable cost to himself, Christ died on a cross to purchase us out of the world for himself. What the cross symbolizes is that we belong to him and not to the world because of the purchase price – the death of Christ.

Making the cross central to our life helps us grasp our priorities in a way that nothing else can. That is why reformation is always along a path that leads back to the cross. A significant aspect of cross wisdom is the reminder that the church is to embrace weakness. This is in total opposition to the way of the world. Paul modelled this remarkably. If anyone had reasons for self-promotion, he did. I cannot think of a Christian celebrity today with a more impressive bio than this super apostle. He had the best education money could buy. Tarsus was renowned as an academic centre of the Roman world, so Paul had the equivalent of Oxbridge or Ivy League schooling. He also had the great rabbi Gamaliel as his personal supervisor. Examine his writing and you see a genius to match the smartest people who ever lived. He is right up there with Robert Oppenheimer and Albert Einstein, the theoretical physicists who pioneered the atomic bomb.

Among Paul's list of achievements was 'founder of the Christian church in the Roman Empire'. We also know he was a prolific writer. Added to this, Paul was someone who moved in the higher echelons of Roman society. If Paul had a blog or Twitter account, all these credentials and achievements would attract a huge following.

But because he was cross-wise, Paul took another tack. He lays this out in 1 Corinthians 1:

For the message of the cross is foolishness to those who are perishing, but to us who are being saved it is the power of God. For it is written:

'I will destroy the wisdom of the wise;
    the intelligence of the intelligent I will frustrate.'

Where is the wise person? Where is the teacher of the law? Where is the philosopher of this age? Has not God made foolish the wisdom of the world? For since in the wisdom of God the world through its wisdom did not know him, God was pleased through the foolishness of what was preached to save those who believe. Jews demand signs and Greeks look for wisdom, but we preach Christ crucified: a stumbling block to Jews and foolishness to Gentiles, but to those whom God has called, both Jews and Greeks, Christ the power of God and the wisdom of God. For the foolishness of God is wiser than human wisdom, and the weakness of God is stronger than human strength.

Brothers and sisters, think of what you were when you were called. Not many of you were wise by human standards; not many were influential; not many were of noble birth. But God chose the foolish things of the world to shame the wise; God chose the weak things of the world to shame the strong. God chose the lowly things of this world and the despised things – and the things that are not – to nullify the things that are, so that no one may boast before him. It is because of him that you are in Christ Jesus, who has become for us wisdom from God – that is, our righteousness, holiness and redemption. Therefore, as it is written: 'Let the one who boasts boast in the Lord.'
(1 Cor. 1:18–31)

Returning to the cross will reform the church because it will restore us to the way of weakness. Here is how we reflect being an unworldly people. It is a path so incongruous to the way of the world, which endorses strength, status and being impressive. For Paul, the cross put all that to death, which is why he said the world was crucified to him.

Today, the church is being forced to the way of weakness. After holding a position of cultural power for so long, we are now a beleaguered minority. On occasions when I am at the Emirates to see Arsenal play, I get a sense of this. Here I am in a packed stadium with 64,000 passionate worshippers of a great contest. Others would love to be there but couldn't get a ticket. The next day in church there I am with a handful of worshippers, and it is not standing-room only.

The church does not impress the world, and that is OK. As a cross-wise people, we can even embrace our beleaguered position as a mark of the cross on us. When the early church began, it had no status, no heritage to point to – just small groups of believers with a clear confession, a strong binding and a willingness to be reproached for Christ's sake.

Europe is the first continent in history to go through the double process of Christianization and de-Christianization. We are now back in the space the early church occupied. That is our opportunity to make the cross our boast and to plot a different course from the world. Allowing the cross to shape us will make a nonsense of our Christian celebrity culture, our corporatization and our turning everything into fast-food outlets. With the cross at the centre, we have nothing to prove to the world except the way of humility. Our confession, our worship and our community mark us – not the glitz and the glamour and the noise.

A revived church

It is my conviction that our present malaise is so great that the church cannot reform its way out of it. That is why we need to call on the Lord to revive us. We have already noted that this is not something we can do for ourselves. Without an outpouring of the Spirit, it is unlikely that much will change. And revival will make no sense to us unless we see our need of it. To acknowledge that we need reviving is to admit something is amiss. Many churches today do not even have a category for what revival is. That itself is telling and symptomatic of our crisis of worldliness. We must become revival-conscious.

Becoming revival-conscious is important because it puts the focus in the right place. Today, the church's concern with culture has made us social critics, diverting us from the real problem. We look at current affairs and bristle with indignation at the godlessness. To be revival-conscious shifts the spotlight back to us. Revival is not something that can happen to the world because the world can't be resuscitated. As the New Testament reflects, everything outside Christ is spiritually dead. You wouldn't give the kiss of life to a corpse. That situation requires resurrection – not resuscitation.

Christ filling his temple

This resuscitation happens when Christ fills the church with his light and life. For that reason, I like to see revival as analogous to what happened to Solomon's temple. After monumental industry and effort, the splendid structure was complete. One detail remained unfinished: the God of Israel had yet to take up residence there. King Solomon was keen for this to happen so every spectator would be in no doubt God had come home. That is why he prayed:

> Now arise, LORD God, and come to your resting place,
>   you and the ark of your might.
> May your priests, LORD God, be clothed with salvation,
>   may your faithful people rejoice in your goodness.
> LORD God, do not reject your anointed one.
>   Remember the great love promised to David your servant.
> (2 Chr. 6:41–42)

What came next must have exceeded his expectation. We are told:

> When Solomon finished praying, fire came down from heaven and consumed the burnt offering and the sacrifices, and the glory of the LORD filled the temple. The priests could not enter the temple of the LORD because the glory of the LORD filled it. When all the Israelites saw the fire coming down and the glory of the LORD above the temple, they knelt on the pavement with their faces to the ground, and they worshiped and gave thanks to the LORD, saying,
>
> 'He is good;
> his love endures forever.
> (2 Chr. 7:1–3)

It was a divine drama, nothing less than spectacular – the fire and the glory and a blazing light to blind the eye.

When revival happens, Christ doesn't smuggle himself in via the back door. Rather, he makes his descent in power and glory. It may lack the visuals of what Solomon witnessed, but it is still unmistakable. No more holograms, no more whipped-up excitement from the band, but the reality of Jesus in the centre of his people. Then, worship time is spontaneous. It doesn't need to be choreographed because the group breaks into song, 'He is good; his love endures forever.' He is so real, we just know that it's all about him and not about us. And sentimentality isn't possible.

Revival is about reality, the reality of Christ – deeper than anything we have experienced. This reorders our affections. Now we know our supreme good because he is with us. Such a sight also strengthens our allegiance. Now we have seen him, the thought of being unfaithful is unthinkable – even when this hurts.

And so this is what the righteous must do – become two-legged. As we reform, we do this with a profound revival consciousness. That means us doing our part even as we look to Christ and his Spirit to do his.

Christ the winnower will make his church good

In a time of decline, it is tempting to live in negativity and gloom. With Christ in our vision, we can avoid this. Jesus promises us in Matthew 16:18, 'I will build my church, and the gates of Hades will not overcome it.' As the One who purchased us by his death on the cross, he is committed to making us good. The church is not tasked with building the church; he is – and nothing will stop it happening.

Christ is committed to our purity, and that is why he is the divine winnower. Winnowing is the agricultural process to remove the chaff so only the grain head remains. Throughout the history of his church, when the chaff and the dust have built up, Christ the winnower has gone to work. He shakes things up so the church is renewed and restored.

Christ commits to making us a holy people uncontaminated by the world's values. When these get embedded in the church's life, it becomes necessary for him to sift us. This occurred back in the nineteenth century when a wave of liberal thought swept through Protestant churches. This gutted the faith by denying 'mere Christianity', discarding basic doctrines such as Christ's divinity, the miracles and the resurrection. It was all very fashionable and respectable, but from where we stand today we can see the winnowing effect. The landscapes of Europe and North America are littered with former church buildings used now as restaurants and offices – a divine winnowing.

There are signs of another winnowing today. Our culture of celebrities and Christian superstars appears to be in the threshing chamber. Many have fallen from their pedestals and been exposed for hypocrisy. Something is shaking the church. We do not know what the fallout will be, but it feels as if a winnowing has begun. If that is true, then we must allow ourselves to be open to questions.

For those comfortably inside the church, now is a moment to seriously reflect on our present disorder. We must address what pursuing reformation and asking God for revival should look like in our corporate lives. For those wary of church, I hope you see that many of your concerns are validated. Despite the church's problems, I encourage you to commit to a fellowship where Christ is central, however imperfectly. In such places, one hopes that leaders will be open to discussion about areas where the church may be worldly.

Living as a hopeful people

It is a scary moment for the church, and what our future holds is beyond us to fathom. It could be that in the coming few decades we will see a great falling away. That has already occurred in Europe, so maybe America with its high church attendance could also see a culling. As bad as it gets, we do not need to panic. No doubt the Secular Age is a colossus with its influence and power. But then again, Rome with all its power could not domesticate the early Christians to its agenda. And they, like us, had a minority status. Because of Christ's promise, we know that the church will never be destroyed, and in him our cause will triumph in the end. That is our guarantee and the basis for being a hopeful people – and we have every reason to hope. And a reason to hope is a reason to live.

Christians should never be a people of negativity and despair, crying into our teacups how dreadful it all is. We have a basis in Christ right now to live fully. This is not the positivity of the world – a 'fake it till you make it'. We don't have to whip life up by creating excitement. No – Christ is ours and that is enough. With him before us, we have everything to live for. To be his unworldly people in an age of decline is our opportunity to embrace the life we have been given.

Let's remember the treatment – remembering Jesus for who he is and smuggling him back into church and into the heart of our own lives. Christ is both supremely powerful and supremely beautiful, and this can crack open the horizons of our egoism (chapter 3). He is Creator of all that is seen and unseen, the giver of all good things we enjoy, and seeing this lifts our eyes from a naturalistic outlook (chapter 4). Christ is our supreme good, the One who gives true joy and meaning to life (chapter 5). And Christ is Lord of all creation, the One who will establish his kingdom of justice and peace when he returns – we must be loyal to him above the cultural pressures on us and the temptations to worldly relevance and power (chapter 6).

And so we live in the wider horizon he gives us, and as we live, live, live, we call out, 'Maranatha – Come, Lord Jesus, Come.' And he will come, because he loves his church and is committed to completing what he has begun.

Chapter summary

The contemporary evangelical church has become worldly through accommodating the secular values of the world around us. A key question for the church today is provided by Psalm 11:3: 'When the foundations are being destroyed, what can the righteous do?' The answer is to look to Christ on his heavenly throne. Rather than tampering with structures and externals, the way out of being worldly is to see him and know him for who he really is. To become what we are with a radical Christlike distinctiveness requires both reformation and revival. Reformation is what the church must do, and this requires demolishing strongholds and strengthening the things that remain. Revival is what Christ does in the power of his Spirit to revitalize us. This comes as a shaking both to rescue us from the world and to restore us to our centre in him.

Questions

- When was the last time your experience of the Bible was Christ speaking to you?
- How can an 'orthodoxy of community' be nurtured in the church you are part of?
- What practical steps can your church take to develop a revival consciousness?

Further reading

Martyn Lloyd-Jones, *Revival* (Wheaton, Ill: Crossway, 1987).

Ian J. Shaw, *Lessons from Old Masters on Evangelicals and Social Action: From John Wesley to John Stott* (London: IVP, 2021).

Abraham Kuyper, *Lectures on Calvinism* (Georgia: Dallas Books, 2018).

Timothy Ward, *Words of Life: Scripture as the Living and Active Word of God* (Nottingham: IVP, 2009).

Acknowledgments

This book would never have seen the light of day were it not for my wife, Helen. She was my constant encourager and cast her keen editorial eye over early drafts of each chapter. My gratitude to her is unbounded.

Thank you also to Steve Midgley, who commissioned me to preach a sermon series at Christ Church Cambridge on the subject of 'Culture Matters'. Undertaking that proved to be the genesis for this book.

Many hours of conversations with close friends whose vocation is directly tied to the church have also been invaluable, with special thanks to Gavin McGrath, Mark Meynell, Marsh Moyle and Mark Stirling. I am also grateful to David Illman, whose personal encouragement and sharp eye with regard to cultural trends were a stimulus and help.

It would be hard to overstate my appreciation for Caleb Woodbridge, IVP's publishing director. Our partnership in the final crafting of this book was literally a godsend.

It would be remiss of me not to mention the many students who sought asylum at L'Abri after harmful experiences in their home churches. Your lamentations did not go unheard and were instructive in helping me discern the deeper problems.

Finally, I must thank my parents, who modelled from the beginning what a Christ-centred existence looks like.

As Johann Sebastian Bach wrote the initials 'S.D.G.' at the end of many of his compositions, so I end mine with the same. *Soli Deo gloria* – Glory to God alone!